COMMUNITY
and Quality of Life
DATA NEEDS FOR
INFORMED DECISION MAKING

Committee on Identifying Data Needs for Place-Based Decision Making
Committee on Geography
Board on Earth Sciences and Resources
Division on Earth and Life Studies
National Research Council

NATIONAL ACADEMY PRESS
Washington, D.C.

NATIONAL ACADEMY PRESS • 2101 Constitution Ave., N.W. • Washington, DC 20418

NOTICE: The project that is the subject of this report was approved by the Governing Board of the National Research Council, whose members are drawn from the councils of the National Academy of Sciences, the National Academy of Engineering, and the Institute of Medicine. The members of the committee responsible for the report were chosen for their special competences and with regard for appropriate balance.

This study was supported by an agreement between the National Academy of Sciences and the U.S. Department of Transportation. Any opinions, findings, conclusions, or recommendations expressed in this publication are those of the author(s) and do not necessarily reflect the view of the organizations or agencies that provided support for this project.

Library of Congress Cataloging-in-Publication Data

Community and quality of life : data needs for informed decision making
/ Committee on Identifying Data Needs for Place-Based Decision Making ;
Committee on Geography.
    p. cm.
Includes bibliographical references and index.
 ISBN 0-309-08260-9 (Hardcover)
 1. Quality of life—United States. 2. Quality of life—United
States—Decision making. 3. Community development, Urban—United
States—Citizen participation. 4. Transportation—United
States—Planing—Citizen participation. I. National Research Council
(U.S.). Committee on Identifying Data Needs for Place-Based Decision
Making. II. National Research Council (U.S.). Committee on Geography.
HN60 .C64 2002
306'.0973—dc21

2002006877

Additional copies of this report are available from:

National Academy Press.
2101 Constitution Ave., N.W.
Box 285
Washington, DC 20055
800-624-6242
202-334-3313 (in the Washington Metropolitan Area)
http://www.nap.edu

Cover: Background: Plans, metropolitan highway radials, Boston, Mass., courtesy of the Frances Loeb Library Graduate School of Design, Harvard University.
Foreground: Playing Children, courtesy of PhotoDisc, Inc.; Town Square, Woodstock, Ill., 1941, photograph by John Vachon; Forest Hills Garden, sketch: Station Square, Forest Hills, Long Island (Borough of Queens), N.Y., 1910, courtesy of the Frances Loeb Library Graduate School of Design, Harvard University.

Printed in the United States of America

THE NATIONAL ACADEMIES

National Academy of Sciences
National Academy of Engineering
Institute of Medicine
National Research Council

The **National Academy of Sciences** is a private, nonprofit, self-perpetuating society of distinguished scholars engaged in scientific and engineering research, dedicated to the furtherance of science and technology and to their use for the general welfare. Upon the authority of the charter granted to it by the Congress in 1863, the Academy has a mandate that requires it to advise the federal government on scientific and technical matters. Dr. Bruce M. Alberts is president of the National Academy of Sciences.

The **National Academy of Engineering** was established in 1964, under the charter of the National Academy of Sciences, as a parallel organization of outstanding engineers. It is autonomous in its administration and in the selection of its members, sharing with the National Academy of Sciences the responsibility for advising the federal government. The National Academy of Engineering also sponsors engineering programs aimed at meeting national needs, encourages education and research, and recognizes the superior achievements of engineers. Dr. Wm. A. Wulf is president of the National Academy of Engineering.

The **Institute of Medicine** was established in 1970 by the National Academy of Sciences to secure the services of eminent members of appropriate professions in the examination of policy matters pertaining to the health of the public. The Institute acts under the responsibility given to the National Academy of Sciences by its congressional charter to be an adviser to the federal government and, upon its own initiative, to identify issues of medical care, research, and education. Dr. Harvey V. Fineberg is president of the Institute of Medicine.

The **National Research Council** was organized by the National Academy of Sciences in 1916 to associate the broad community of science and technology with the Academy's purposes of furthering knowledge and advising the federal government. Functioning in accordance with general policies determined by the Academy, the Council has become the principal operating agency of both the National Academy of Sciences and the National Academy of Engineering in providing services to the government, the public, and the scientific and engineering communities. The Council is administered jointly by both Academies and the Institute of Medicine. Dr. Bruce M. Alberts and Dr. Wm. A. Wulf are chairman and vice chairman, respectively, of the National Research Council.

COMMITTEE ON IDENTIFYING DATA NEEDS FOR PLACE-BASED DECISION MAKING

KATHLEEN E. STEIN, *Chair,* Howard/Stein-Hudson Associates, Inc., Boston, Massachusetts
ANN AZARI, Ann Azari Consulting, Fort Collins, Colorado
ROGER E. BOLTON, Williams College, Williamstown, Massachusetts
WILLIAM J. CRAIG, University of Minnesota, Minneapolis
ROBERT T. DUNPHY, Urban Land Institute, Washington, D.C.
CHARLES E. HOWARD, Jr., Washington State Department of Transportation, Olympia
RANDY JOHNSON, Hennepin County Board of Commissioners, Hennepin County, Minneapolis, Minnesota
PAUL L. KNOX, Virginia Polytechnic Institute and State University, Blacksburg
HARVEY J. MILLER, University of Utah, Salt Lake City
JENNIFER R. WOLCH, University of Southern California, Los Angeles

National Research Council Staff

LISA M. VANDEMARK, Study Director
MONICA R. LIPSCOMB, Research Assistant (from May 2001)
SUSAN B. MOCKLER, Research Associate (September 2000 to March 2001)
VERNA J. BOWEN, Administrative Assistant

Acknowledgments

This report has been reviewed in draft form by individuals chosen for their diverse perspectives and technical expertise, in accordance with procedures approved by the National Research Council's Report Review Committee. The purpose of this independent review is to provide candid and critical comments that will assist the institution in making its published report as sound as possible and to ensure that the report meets institutional standards for objectivity, evidence, and responsiveness to the study charge. The review comments and draft manuscript remain confidential to protect the integrity of the deliberative process. We wish to thank the following individuals for their review of this report:

Carl Abbott, Urban Studies and Planning, Portland State University, Portland, Oregon
Jonathan Barnett, Independent Consultant, Washington, D.C.
Bruce Cahan, Urban Logic, Inc. New York, New York
Deborah Knopman, RAND, Arlington, Virginia
Keith Laughlin, Rails-to-Trails Conservancy, Washington, D.C.

Although the reviewers listed above have provided many constructive comments and suggestions, they were not asked to endorse the conclusions or recommendations nor did they see the final draft of the report before its release. The review of this report was overseen by Dr. Susan Cutter, University of South Carolina, Columbia. Appointed by the

National Research Council, she was responsible for making certain that an independent examination of this report was carried out in accordance with institutional procedures and that all review comments were carefully considered. Responsibility for the final content of this report rests entirely with the authoring committee and the institution.

In addition, we wish to thank the participants in the Workshop on Transportation Decision Making: Place, Community, and Quality of Life that was held at the Arnold and Mabel Beckman Center in Irvine, California, on January 27-29, 2001. These participants' names are listed in Appendix B. Several of the participants presented case histories at the workshop that are included in this report. For contributing to the development of case studies presented in this report, the committee thanks Stacy Fehlenberg, U.S. Environmental Protection Agency, Atlanta, Georgia; Dennis Goreham, Automated Geographic Research Center, Salt Lake City, Utah; Natalie Gochnour, Demographic & Economic Analysis, Salt Lake City, Utah; Jacky Grimshaw, Center for Neighborhood Technology; Transportation and Air Quality Programs, Chicago, Illinois; Bob Nagel, Automated Geographic Research Center, Salt Lake City, Utah; Carol Swenson, University of Minnesota, Minneapolis; Hannah Twaddell, Thomas Jefferson Planning District Commission, Charlottesville-Albemarle Metropolitan Planning Organization, Charlottesville, Virginia; Dennis Welsch, City of Roseville, Minnesota.

A workshop on federal data provision was held at the National Research Council on February 5, 2001. We thank the following participants: Geoffrey Anderson, U.S. Environmental Protection Agency, Washington, D.C.; Daniel K. Cavanaugh, U.S. Geological Survey, Reston, Virginia; John Eltinge, U.S. Bureau of Land Management, Washington, D.C.; Hugh W. Knox, U.S. Department of Commerce, Washington, D.C.; Richard Reeder, U.S. Department of Agriculture, Washington, D.C.; U.S. Census Bureau, Washington, D.C.; Leo B. Dougherty, U.S. Census Bureau, Washington, D.C.; David E. Chase, U.S. Department of Housing and Urban Development, Washington, D.C.; Paul Dresler, U.S. Department of the Interior, Washington, D.C.; and Stacy Fehlenberg, U.S. Environmental Protection Agency, Atlanta, Georgia.

The committee also expresses its gratitude to other individuals who provided advice and materials for the report. We were assisted by Katherine Wallman, chief statistician, Office of Management and Budget; Andrew Reamer, principal, Andrew Reamer and Associates; Keith Laughlin, director, and Christopher Thomson, associate director, of Vice-President Gore's White House Task Force on Livable Communities; Robert Sloane, senior planner, Howard/Stein-Hudson Associates; Michael Meyer, professor, School of Civil and Environmental Engineering, Georgia Institute of Technology; Roy Sparrow, professor of public administration, Robert F.

Wagner School of Public Service, New York University; and Tom Palmerlee, senior program officer, Transportation Research Board, National Research Council.

We are grateful for the assistance of the National Research Council staff in organizing the study and preparing the report. Staff members who contributed to this effort are Lisa M. Vandemark, study director and staff director of the Committee on Geography; Susan Mockler, research associate; Monica Lipscomb, research assistant and author of the case studies; and Verna Bowen, administrative associate. For preparation and editing of the final report, we also thank Shannon Ruddy, Winfield Swanson, and Teresia Wilmore.

Preface

In recent decades, dramatic changes have taken place in the nature of information, analyses, decision tools and processes, and the core considerations that go into transportation decision making. This expansion of scope and the profound democratization of planning and decision-making processes have created new requirements for data and associated analytical and decision-support tools. One challenge that has emerged is how to capture and reflect the complex interrelationships between transportation and the social, economic, land use, and environmental contexts of host communities so as to incorporate these into thoughtful decision making that will support, rather than harm, the livability of communities. A related challenge is how to meet the needs of diverse stakeholders, including planners and analysts who develop and assess both regional system-level transportation plans and potential project investments; public officials, charged with decision responsibilities but often lacking technical expertise in the disciplines that go into the analysis of decision choices; and community members and interest groups who care about the livability of their places, which are significantly impacted by transportation facilities and services.

In proposing this project to the National Research Council (NRC), the U.S. Department of Transportation's Bureau of Transportation Statistics (BTS) sought to meet the significant and growing need for more informed consideration of the complex and interrelated impacts of transportation decisions on the livability of communities. This effort was carried out under the auspices of the Committee on Geography of NRC's Board on

Earth Sciences and Resources. The National Research Council charged the project committee with identifying the data and measures needed to make local and regional public decisions on transportation, land use planning, and economic development that aim to enhance "livability." The committee was both inspired and challenged by a topic of such breadth and significance. The resulting work draws upon a wide body of knowledge and practice in disciplines ranging from geography to transportation planning, engineering, environmental analysis, and the economic, social, and political sciences.

One early issue that the committee revisited throughout its work was how to honor the broad scope of the topic while producing findings and recommendations that would be specific enough to be helpful to transportation planners, community members, and decision makers. In order to achieve this goal, the committee examined the concept of livable communities, the selection of livability indicators, and the means of measuring these indicators. Committee members also provided information on the use and availability of these data for public decision making. Additionally, the committee identified opportunities for meeting data needs at the federal level and reviewed the plans of federal agencies to make needed data available to the public.

Although much work remains to be done, the committee hopes that this report fulfills the expectations of its sponsors and aids all participants in the transportation decision process. We commend the wisdom and foresight of the Bureau of Transportation Statistics in requesting this study and in providing financial support to carry it out. In certain sections of this report, the committee focused on transportation in order to respond to the concerns and needs highlighted by BTS. Similar attention might be given to other major elements of public infrastructure, including water supply, because the issue of impacts on the livability of communities is equally germane there.

In addition to the acknowledgments, I extend my heartfelt thanks to Lisa Vandemark, our study director, who contributed wise guidance and hard work at every step along the way, and to the committee members who gave generously of their expertise, energy, and insights in researching this topic and preparing the following report.

Kathleen E. Stein
Chair

Contents

Executive Summary

Communities across the nation are faced with difficult and complex decisions about how to respond to change, plan sensibly, and improve the quality of life for all of their members. Suburban communities are dealing with sprawl that threatens the qualities of greenness and space that initially attracted residents. Cities struggle to revitalize urban centers without displacing existing communities and cultures. Rural communities strive to balance traditional ways of life with the need for access to jobs, health care, and education. More and more, people demand a voice in what happens in their communities and an active role in deciding what, where, and how change occurs.

In order to participate meaningfully in this process of decision making and to make well-informed decisions affecting quality of life, communities need information from specialized data and from decision-support tools that assess the implications of alternatives. The extent to which available data and tools can be used by communities to make these complex decisions, spanning the interrelated domains of economy, environment, and society, has rarely been examined. The Bureau of Transportation Statistics (BTS) of the U.S. Department of Transportation (DOT) asked the National Research Council to conduct this assessment, in support of multiple efforts on the part of government at all levels and of citizen groups, to encourage broad and effective public participation in the planning of livable communities.

This report focuses on the range of data needed by communities to plan and participate in decisions that affect the quality of life in those communities, as well as the range of data needed for making transportation decisions that support community livability. Data needed by communities involved in decision making might include both socioeconomic and environmental statistics. Transportation data for sound decision making related to the broader goal of planning livable communities can come from a variety of sources ranging from local to national and spanning the public and private sectors.

The committee's formal statement of task was as follows:

> The committee will convene a workshop to identify the data, including geo-spatial data, and performance measures needed to make local and regional decisions on transportation, land use planning, and economic development. Based on the results of the workshop, the committee will undertake the following additional tasks: (1) review the availability and usefulness of data and performance measures to enhance "livability" or quality of life; (2) identify opportunities for meeting data needs and improving the decision-support systems; and (3) review the plans of federal agencies for developing these measures and making needed data available to the public.

To honor the breadth of the charge within its time and resource constraints, the committee decided to examine the idea of livability as a goal for communities; to discuss issues surrounding the choice of livability indicators and the measurement of those characteristics; and to provide information on the use and availability of relevant data for public decision making. Additionally, the committee identified opportunities for meeting data needs and improving decision-support systems, and reviewed the plans of federal agencies for making needed data available to the public.

Performance indicators rely on many of the same data and types of data that the committee discussed in detail, in terms of identifying indicators of livability. Choosing among possible performance measures is similar to choosing among sets of indicators; indeed, performance measures must be defined in terms of the indicators of change that they mean to measure. Proper performance measures and appropriate and useful decision-support tools vary with the community and the project.

This report offers general guidelines about the qualities and characteristics that define well-considered measures and tools, as well as an appendix on federal data sources describing the range of current research on community-based performance measures of livability and decision-support tools for increasing public participation in planning.

The 1990s marked a surge in societal interest in planning and building livable communities and a growing commitment on the part of the federal government to provide the support and information that communities need for sustainable development. At the local, state, and federal levels, efforts were geared toward the inclusion in the decision-making process of all people who live and work in these communities. Further, citizen participation was encouraged from start to finish in the complex process of making decisions that affect the quality of life in communities. This was in sharp contrast to the kinds of participatory planning that brought in stakeholders only after major agendas had been set, thus reducing the influence of stakeholders on the end results.

During the same period, there was an increase in publicly available data. However, it became clear that data alone, without decision-support tools to help people use these data, would not lead to an increase in public participation in the decision-making process. At the same time, community efforts were launched across the country to identify indicators of livability.

Livability is an ensemble concept whose factors include or relate to a number of other complex characteristics or states, including sustainability, quality of both life and place, and healthy communities (Norris and Pittman, 2000; Blassingame, 1998). It is the more immediate manifestation of sustainability that, like livability, refers to the ability of a place or a community to meet the needs of its current citizens without compromising the ability of future generations to meet their full range of human needs.

Although the definition of livability varies from community to community, a given community's goals can be approached, and community planning for livability can be achieved, using community-derived indicators. Often, the initial goal for people involved in the planning process is to determine what is important in and to the community.

Data must be available to measure these indicators, and many, but not all, of the needed data are spatial in nature, involving relationships between places, such as home and school, city and region, and issues of space, such as percentage of open space or space-time, including emergency response time. The range of possible indicators is wide, but a balanced set will include indicators from the social, environmental, and economic sectors. A few examples among many alternatives include economic indicators, such as whether jobs pay living wages, come with health insurance and retirement benefits, are close to affordable transit and child care, and provide safe working environments. Social indicators might include community involvement (e.g., volunteerism), number of community gardens, distance between residences of extended family members, access to health care, and equity (diversity, employment types, etc.). Examples of place-based environmental indicators include measures of species diversity, land use, soil type, surface water, wetlands, and so forth. Transportation indicators include data on built infrastructure, the percentage of the population commuting a particular distance, the percentage using public transit versus personal vehicles, and alternatively, the number of pedestrian-friendly streets, ratio of bike paths to streets, and percentage of street miles designated as bike route miles. The key is to achieve balance among social, environmental, and economic indicators and to attend to the interrelationships among these indicators.

Conclusions and recommendations in this report derive from the following:

1. a review of the availability and usefulness of data and performance measures to enhance livability or quality of life;
2. an assessment of the opportunities to meet the data needs of the public and to improve the decision-support systems for applying these data to decision making;
3. a review of the plans of federal agencies for developing these measures and making needed data available to the public.

The task presented to this committee was broad, encompassing identification of the data and measures needed to make local and regional public decisions on transportation, land use planning, and economic development that aim to enhance livability or quality of life. The committee determined early in the study process that an understanding of "place" was fundamental to thinking about livability, especially transportation-related aspects of livability. Connections between people and places are complex and difficult to measure. To guide the study process and to frame the committee's conclusions and recommendations, fundamental geographic concepts were applied. These concepts can also help guide communities as they make complex decisions that require an understanding of spatial relationships and the mutual dependence of social, economic, and environmental systems. The concepts of place, scale, and the importance of people-place interactions are traditional geographic perspectives and are discussed in the Introduction and in Chapter 2.

While the specific set of indicators chosen by a community will be the product of numerous factors including demographics, region, historical precedents, and the nature of the decision or project planned, the data needed fall into three main categories: (1) social data, (2) environmental data, and (3) economic data. A major conclusion of this study is that the basic economic, social, and environmental dimensions of livability are not completely separable from each other. For example, environmental health cannot be traded-off against social well-being or vice versa; each depends upon the other. The key is their mutual interdependence. Selected indicators of livability must span these sectors, and some indicators must cut across these sectors.

Dimensions of livability operate at multiple, interconnected spatial and temporal scales. For data on livability to be useful, they must be integrated to reflect interdependence among people and places, between places, among scales (especially between community and regional levels), and among sectors (social, environmental, and economic). Indicators must be measured in ways that are sensitive to these interactive processes and to change over time, so historical data become important.

The analysis of livability of a place is strongly influenced by the geographic unit of measurement chosen, for example, census tract, school district, municipality, or watershed. Scale and zoning are two dimensions of the spatial aggregation of data for any particular analysis. Problems associated with the arbitrary nature of chosen geographic units are discussed as the modifiable area unit problem (MAUP) in Chapter 3.

Finally, although public data are useful for decision making, improvements in data availability are necessary and decision-support tools must be designed for the use of diverse stakeholders. This group includes individuals and representatives of government, the private sector, and community-based groups who are involved in planning livable communities nationwide. Efforts are going on to create opportunities for data sharing among federal agencies, for partnerships with state and local governments to enhance the public data available for common programs, and for new efforts in coordination. In order to coordinate with other agencies, not only the will, but also the permission and appropriate funding, are necessary. Each federal agency carries specific and critical responsibilities to serve the interests of the nation. Collection, analysis, and reporting of data and information are designed primarily to support these unique and critical national missions. Opportunities exist for multiagency cooperation in areas of mutual interest; these could enhance the ability of the government to serve the public in terms of data and information needs.

The major conclusions of the committee and recommendations for improving data availability, including access and applicability, are summarized below:

Basic dimensions of livability are not completely separable or mutually compensatory. Livability concepts often treat economic, social, and environmental factors as separate domains that can be traded against each other. This leads to issue-specific planning efforts (e.g., by economic development organizations) that pay far too little attention to the web of interconnections among these dimensions. Transportation policies of the past have been criticized for such single-issue focus. The Interstate Highway System, for example, had a clear focus on linking major cities but a blindness toward the effect of changes on neighborhoods adjacent to the highways. This created "freeway revolts" in San Francisco, New Orleans, and other affected cities. In another example, planning emphases on protecting urban parklands and historic areas have been viewed as primarily serving the economically advantaged while a broader environmental justice approach to siting roads and other infrastructure brings more attention to low-income and minority populations. The environment is the most fundamental matrix for livability, and environmental and social quality of life are important components of economic well-being if the latter is measured correctly. Consequently, the nature of trade-offs among social, environmental, and economic dimensions is much less clear in the long run than it may appear in the short run.

Crosscutting measures of livability that highlight the mutual interdependence of livability dimensions are essential. Political debates often focus on which goals to pursue and assume that progress on one front will necessarily mean a loss on another front; the result is classic "environment-versus-economy" disputes. In the long run, environmental degradation will make the economy falter. Environmental and social quality of life are seen as important components of economic well-being if the latter is measured not in terms of simple indicators such as Gross National Product (GNP), but with more nuanced measures that relate how well the economy is meeting the complex needs of society. Location, for example, is an important, crosscutting aspect of livability. In the context of transportation decision making, the value of location can be presented in comprehensible terms by the use of off-the-shelf statistical software packages that calculate for any place the number of nearby opportunities, such as food stores or green spaces, or the distance to the nearest medical facility or bus stop. A good example of a complex crosscutting measure is the ecological footprint described in Box 1.1.

Dimensions of livability operate at multiple interconnected spatial scales and time frames. Livability is perceived and experienced by people who live, work, or recreate in particular places; yet our decisions about how to live influence the livability of larger regions and even distant places and people. Moreover, our current decisions about a single place at one point in time—about life-styles, transportation choices, and environmental amenities—affect the livability of multiple places over different scales (e.g., region, nation, globe) and over time.

Data on both people and places are fundamental for assessing livability. People and place are the two sides of livability, but livability indicators often refer only to locality or territory, rather than to individuals (especially as they change and move over time). Neither type of indicator captures the full picture of livability. Moreover, reliance on information about only people or localities can be seriously misleading. For example, tracking aggregate community income over time in a specific locality might show rising economic well-being, but this could be because gentrification has displaced lower-income people who have been thrust into more congested, affordable housing markets. Improving a place at the expense of other places can result in net loss of social, economic, and environmental quality. Thus, both people and place-based indicators are fundamental to the understanding and measurement of livability.

Each federal data program has been developed for carrying out agency-specific missions, yet all federal agencies carry critical responsibilities to serve the interests of the nation. The collection, analysis, and reporting of data and information are designed primarily to support these unique and critical federal missions. At the same time, it is recognized that other levels of government also collect and utilize data for public policy purposes. Cooperation in areas of mutual interest could enhance the ability of all agencies of government to serve the public in this regard. Several projects in this spirit have been initiated by the federal government (e.g., see the discussion of the Geodata Alliance in Chapter 5 and of the Federal Geographic Data Committee [FGDC] in Appendix A), but efforts are still in the beginning stages of development. The potential remains for enhancing relationships and common efforts in data programs.

The committee recommends the following for the improvement of data availability and decision-support systems that will encourage broad public participation in the decision-making process and result in more livable communities:

Livability planning can occur at multiple spatial scales but should be integrated across such scales, especially community-based and regional levels. Livability planning efforts often range from the scale of an entire state, down to small-scale neighborhoods. Data integrated across scales are rare despite the fact that some aspects of livability (e.g., walkability) are experienced mostly at the local scale, whereas others (e.g., air quality) are remediated at the regional scale. A regional-scale livability plan can ensure fair-share distribution of the costs and benefits of transportation services.

Robust livability indicators require data that are measured and integrated in ways that are sensitive to underlying geographic processes. Basic data to support indicators are often measured at different spatial scales. They are also often measured using zoning systems that are artificial (e.g., Census tracts, counties, municipalities, traffic analysis zones) and/or incompatible. This issue can result in arbitrary and biased livability indicators. Geographic Information System (GIS) tools can be used to assess the sensitivity of indicators to the spatial measurement units and aggregation techniques.

Decision-support tools should be designed explicitly for the diverse stakeholders involved in livability planning. Decision-support data and models are often not available, or lack transparency (i.e., they are difficult for users to understand and evaluate). Diverse stakeholders involved in transportation planning include transportation engineers, who are familiar with data and models, and elected officials and members of citizen organizations, who are less familiar with these matters. Moreover, data and models are often limited to the analysis of land use and transportation, when it is essential to integrate economic, social, and environmental data as well. One measure of the weakness of any model is the extent to which it ignores any one of these dimensions. Model-related strengths and weaknesses, as well as their inherent theoretical assumptions, have to be articulated, and new-generation models must integrate, not only land use and transportation, but also ecological-environmental dynamics (related to pollution and habitat effects) and resulting indicators.

Public data are useful for decision making, but improvements are necessary. Federal data creation and delivery programs have provided much useful information to state and local decision makers. These programs could be improved by making selected data available more frequently, for more parts of the country, and at greater resolution and by making multisectoral (social, environmental, economic), mutually compatible data available. Often public data are collected for places defined as political units. State and local data are useful but could be improved by adopting standards allowing data to be comparable across political boundaries. Much more useful data could be available to decision makers at no or low additional costs if administrative data collected by agencies as part of their day-to-day operations were accessible to others outside those agencies.

Continued efforts are required to create opportunities for data sharing among federal agencies and to open up opportunities for partnerships with state and local governments to enhance the public data available for common programs or for new efforts in coordination. Research into the potential expanded use of various federal data sources, specifically for the purposes of cross-discipline public policy issues, is necessary. Exploring what support, what standards, and what controls are needed, as well as how to finance such efforts, may provide a firm base for challenging the separate and individualized systems currently in use. In addition, privacy issues and current regulatory barriers must be addressed. Coordination would be facilitated by clear agency mandates, including appropriate levels of funding to advance such efforts.

REFERENCES

Blassingame, Lurton. 1998. Sustainable cities: oxymoron, utopia, or inevitability? Social Science Journal 35:1-13.

Norris, Tyler, and Mary Pittman. 2000. The health communities movement and the coalition for healthier cities and communities. Public Health Reports 115:118-124.

Introduction

Most Americans conduct their lives within fairly well-defined geographical communities—the territories within which they live, work, and socialize. In each of these communities, decision makers strive to balance competing demands and provide the highest quality of life, or livability, for residents. These decision makers include state and local officials citizens groups, professional planners, and individual citizens.

Transportation agencies too frequently make decisions about transportation investments that give little consideration to the impacts of these investments on the livability of the communities in which they are situated, whether the community is a municipality or a large metropolitan region. Planners, engineers, and decision makers can be so deeply involved in maximizing the transportation-related performance criteria of investments, that trade-offs of that performance goal are not considered, even when these trade-offs are highly relevant to social well-being, as is the reduction of environmental impacts or improved access to services for disadvantaged groups. A broader perspective—supported by appropriate data and decision-support tools—is needed in order to have livability given serious consideration in planning and to have it viewed as a legitimate part of the set of goals to be served by transportation decision making. This effort is hampered by several factors:

1. Addressing the complex issue of livability requires access to a wider variety of information than is traditionally used by the various planning organizations.

2. Communities need to be able to measure whether their actions are improving livability, but they often lack necessary data and face challenges in developing sound methodologies.
3. Organizations and stakeholders often do not have consistent or comparable data, making the analysis of options and decisions more difficult.
4. The information needed to make good decisions may not be available in usable forms.

Better data for transportation planning and decision making will allow consideration of the broad range of real consequences of transportation investments on communities and their members. In addition to considering more narrowly defined transportation consequences—for example, better transit access to major attractions, enhanced goods movement, shorter travel times—improved data will foster more insightful consideration of socioeconomic, land use, and environmental factors that help shape a community's livability. Such factors include mobility and equity consequences across locations within a region and across stakeholder groups; impacts on land use and development patterns, and the consequences of those development patterns; the interaction of transportation operations with the natural and built environments and their impacts on sustainability, distribution of economic benefits and costs both spatially and demographically; and consequences for community cohesiveness.

Technological developments including geographic information systems (GISs) and the Internet have revolutionized the way decision-making data can be collected, analyzed, disseminated, and displayed. Current initiatives on the part of federal, state, and local governments, as well as private and nonprofit groups, to provide such data and to include the broader public in decisions have roots in the social indicators research of the 1930s and 1970s (e.g., Duncan, 1969, 1984; Rossi and Gilmartin, 1980). For example, attempts in the 1960s to understand the roots of poverty reflected the evolution of social views of the root causes and tenacity of poverty. These earlier efforts considered sets of such indicators as socioeconomic status, gender and race, education level, psychological factors, physical characteristics of living conditions, and descriptors of health status (Duncan, 1969). The decade of the 1960s and the early 1970s saw a spike in interest in the federal government for identifying indicators of social well-being and progress (U.S. Department of Health, Education, and Welfare, 1969; OMB, 1973) as part of an effort to understand the relationships between economics and other social sciences (e.g., Olson, 1969).

Previous generations have wrestled with the some of the same questions addressed in this report, for example—the appropriate scale of the indicators, the advantages and limitations of narrow versus crosscutting indicators, and measures of place characteristics versus measures of individual well-being and satisfaction (Land and Spilerman, 1975; Land, 1983). Other research has focused on increasing our understanding of the geographic nature of the relationships that result in quality of life (Cutter, 1985) and has attempted to incorporate environmental variables into livability analyses. More recent efforts have examined quality of life in a national context (e.g., Miringoff, 1999).

However, the current effort differs from past efforts in several respects. First, it focuses on the links between major physical transportation infrastructure and services and the social and economic well-being of communities. Second, it has been prompted by new technologies and data that allow deeper insight into the interactions and causal relationships between public investments in transportation and their effects on individuals, communities, and livability. Third, it grows out of several decades of improvement in transportation planning and decision-making processes that have resulted from legislation and regulation, citizen activism, and pressure for public accountability from transportation agencies and from the application of multidisciplinary skills to consideration of the benefits, costs, and impacts of transportation decisions.

The current effort also grows from a strong interest within public administration and budgeting to develop and use performance indicators and benchmarks. In public sector transportation agencies, such efforts gained momentum in the 1980s and 1990s via implementation of strategic planning and total quality management processes, with their emphasis on measuring performance; responding to customer expectations; and benchmarking, tracking, and reporting results in meeting agency performance goals.

Although the availability of new tools and technologies has changed the way information can be derived and presented, the decision-making process is no less complex. Tools for manipulating disparate types of information, such as GISs, are widely available, but many planners, particularly at the local level, have not yet adopted this capability. Those that have done so may find that their GIS tools are incompatible with the GIS and other analytical tools used by sister planning organizations, which make it difficult to combine data or examine the trade-offs of different planning scenarios.

Finally, planning decisions are made by myriad agencies and organizations, ranging from school boards and state departments of transportation to federal agencies (see Box 1). While this report is aimed at identifying the data that communities need to participate in place-based planning, especially involving transportation decisions, government at all levels from the local to the national plays an essential role in providing support-

---

BOX 1

Government Roles in Transportation Planning

"The federal role in transportation planning is to provide funds, standards, and planning for state and local decision. The states, Metropolitan Planning Organizations (MPOs), and transit operators make project decisions. There are other State, regional, and local rules and requirements affecting transportation decisions . . ." (FHWA, p. 5).

1. State Departments of Transportation are the largest units of government that develop transportation plans and projects. They are responsible for setting the transportation goals for the state. To do so, they work with the state's transportation organizations and local governments. They are responsible for planning safe and efficient transportation between cities and towns in the state.
2. Metropolitan planning organizations (MPOs) represent areas with a population of 50,000 or more. The MPO's mission is to provide short- and long-term solutions to transportation and transportation-related concerns. Local governments carry out many transportation planning functions, such as scheduling improvements and maintenance of local streets and roads.
3. Transit agencies are public and private organizations that provide transportation for the public. Public transportation includes buses, subways, light rail, commuter rail, monorail, passenger ferryboats, trolleys, inclined railways, and other people movers.
4. The U.S. Department of Transportation reviews the transportation planning and project activities of the MPOs and state transportation departments, and supplies critical funding needed for transportation planning and projects. Biannually (at minimum), the federal government approves projects planned by the state departments of transportation and other state agencies using federal funds.

SOURCE: FWHA (no date).

---

ive context for data collection and dissemination and for citizen participation in the decision process. The influence of state departments of transportation, as well as the U.S. Department of Transportation and federal policy such as the National Environmental Policy Act (NEPA), is felt at the community level. Yet these authorities are at times far removed from the specific concerns of a community, and few are sufficiently coordinated to permit cross-organization decision making.

nity is a fundamental element of the sense of place, however, and indeed forms a critical part of the "social capital" of most places.

Moving Through Places. People move into and out of places. Such moves are related to generational and life course changes in the population (e.g., elderly people moving into a nursing home; young families moving into the community). In addition, over time the attraction of any place shifts for particular individuals either as they experience change in personal circumstances or as larger economic, social, or political dynamics remake the place and its opportunities. Therefore, the population composition of any place changes over time, and even if the demographic profile of a place remains stable, the actual individuals who inhabit the place may change over time. Thus, the welfare of places is distinct from that of the people who at some point in time lived or worked there.

Places and Livability

Livability at Multiple Scales. Dimensions of livability operate at multiple interconnected spatial scales and time frames. Livability is a perceived experience by people who live, work, or recreate in particular places; yet decisions about how to live influence the livability of larger regions and even distant places and people. Moreover, our current decisions about a single place at one point in time—about life-styles, transportation choices, and environmental amenities—affect the livability of multiple places over different scales (e.g., region, nation, globe) and times.

Measuring Livability. Data on both individual cohorts of people and the aggregate characteristics of people in particular places are fundamental for assessing livability. People and place are two sides of livability, but livability indicators typically refer only to place and the average profile of residents at one point in time, rather than to individuals as they change and move over time. Neither type of indicator captures the full livability picture. For example, tracking aggregate community income over time in a place might show rising economic well-being and growing retail potential, but this could be only because gentrification has displaced lower-income people who have been thrust into more congested affordable housing markets. It is possible to improve a place and prevent large-scale dislocation of people. Thus, both people- and place-based indicators are fundamental to an understanding and measurement of livability.

Structure of the Report

Chapter 1 discusses the application of the concept of livability or social well-being to planning efforts and the selection and use of livability indicators, and highlights the importance of indicators that crosscut traditional domains of economy, society, and environment. Chapter 2 describes the importance of place and the sense of connectedness that defines communities in the minds of the people who inhabit them. It stresses interconnections between places and among scales, particularly between the regional and the local. Chapter 3 discusses the spatial and temporal issues involved in choosing accurate means of measuring and analyzing livability. Chapter 4 examines the decision process and decision-support systems; and Chapter 5 identifies the data and tools that are required to support sound decision making, that is, to support decisions both that are technically sound and that engage the people impacted by them. Detailed summaries are found at the conclusion of Chapters 3, 4, and 5.

This report is addressed to multiple audiences. Among these are decision makers, from local to national levels, including citizens and citizen groups. Since this report discusses data needs for place-based decision making, another audience includes the federal agencies that provide these data to the public. One strategy for assisting communities in making complex decisions begins with a survey of what data and tools currently exist and where these key data reside. Information relevant to transportation, land-use planning, and economic development can be found in dozens of agencies and organizations, each of which uses different planning aids, ranging from a simple map to state-of-the-art GIS tools. Some of these tools are more effective than others in addressing a specific planning problem, and strategies must include an analysis of how well the various tools perform. Sometimes, it is essential to identify which data and tools for improving decision making are needed but do not exist. For example, rarely do decision-support systems provide adequate means for assessing trade-offs and determining the consequences of a decision. With the right attributes, such systems have the potential for improving decision making and consequently the livability of geographic communities.

Appendix A provides information on the data provision programs and plans of federal agencies and interagency groups, and identifies data sources and decision-support tools available to decision makers and planners. Appendix B summarizes a workshop held as part of the information-gathering phase of the committee's work. Appendix C lists participants in a sub-committee meeting about provision of data by federal agencies. References are made in the text to sources of information on various related topics.

REFERENCES

Cutter, S. L. 1985. Rating Places: A Geographer's View on Quality of Life. Washington D.C: Association of American Geographers Resource Publication.

Duncan, O. D. 1969. Towards Social Reporting: Next Steps. New York: Russell Sage Foundation.

Duncan, O. D. 1984. Notes on Social Measurement, Historical and Critical. Beverly Hills, Calif.: Russell Sage Foundation.

FHWA (Federal Highway Administration). No date. A Citizen's Guide to Transportation Decision Making. Washington, D.C. FHWA publication number FHWA-EP-01-013 HEPH/3-01 (15M)E. Available at http://www.fhwa.dot.gov/planning/citizen/index.htm. Accessed October 8, 2001.

Land, K. C. 1983. Social indicators. Annual Review of Sociology 9:1-26.

Land, K. C., and S. Spilerman. 1975. Social Indicator Models. New York: Russell Sage Foundation.

Miringoff, M. L. 1999. The Social Health of the Nation: How America Is Really Doing. New York: Oxford University Press.

NRC (National Research Council). 1999. Our Common Journey: A Transition Toward Sustainability. Washington, D.C.: National Academy Press. 363 pp.

Olson, Mancur. 1969. The relationships between economics and the other social sciences: The province of a social report. In Seymour Martin Lipset, ed., Politics and the Social Sciences. New York: Oxford University Press.

OMB (Office of Management and Budget). 1973. Social Indicators, 1973: Selected Statistics on Social Conditions and Trends in the United States. Washington, D.C.

Rossi, R. J., and K. J. Gilmartin. 1980. The Handbook of Social Indicators: Sources, Characteristics and Analysis. New York: Garland STPM Press.

U. S. Department of Health, Education, and Welfare. 1969. Toward a Social Report. Washington, D.C.: U.S. Government Printing Office. 101 pp.

Town Square, Woodstock, Ill., 1941. Photograph by John Vachon.

1

Concept of Livability and Indicators

Concept of Livability

"Livability" is a broad term with no precise or universally agreed-upon definition. The concept embraces cognate notions such as sustainability, quality of life, the "character" of place, and the health of communities. Livability is an "ensemble concept" (Myers, 1988; Andrews, 2001) whose factors include many complex characteristics and states. Like the Bruntland Commission's definition of sustainability, the idea of livability includes the ability of a community to meet "the needs of the present without compromising the ability of future generations to meet their own needs" (World Commission on Environment and Development, 1987, p. 23). Sustainability underscores the demand for intergenerational equity and recognizes the limits set by ecological conditions such as the finite nature of certain natural resources like fossil fuels.

Livability encompasses broad human needs ranging from food and basic security to beauty, cultural expression, and a sense of belonging to a community or a place. "Quality of life" emerged as a concept within the Social Indicators Movement of the 1960s and questioned basic assumptions about the relationship between economic and social well-being and the complex nature of individual and social material and immaterial well-being. Quality of life might refer to a citizen's satisfaction with residential environments, traffic, crime rate, employment opportunities, or the amount of open space (Myers, 1988). Alternatively, the phrase might refer to less tangible qualities such as freedom of expression and social justice (Land, 1996). Character of place considers some of these same attributes as bundles of features linked to particular places (e.g., how a community's health is affected by air quality or access to health services).

Together, the concepts of sustainability and livability help us to consider the quality of life for all members of a community or residents of a place, and how the activities and choices of these individuals will impact on the lives of future generations. A sustainable community would not be built on consumptive practices that cannot be maintained over two generations; one livable community cannot be maintained at the expense of its neighbors (a socially costly example of environmental injustice is the siting of waste facilities in economically disadvantaged areas). Using livability or sustainability as a key word, many good sources of information and examples of community-derived indicators of livability can be found on the Internet. Many communities post their choice of indicators, and these can serve as examples for other communities. (Information-rich sites include Sustainable Measures [http://sustainablemeasures.com] and the Smart Growth Network [http://smartgrowth.org].)

The idea of livability bridges many of the other concepts discussed in this section. It refers to the extent to which the attributes of a particular place can, as they interact with one another and with activities in other places, satisfy residents by meeting their economic, social, and cultural needs, promoting their health and well-being, and protecting natural resources and ecosystem functions. As a crosscutting concept, livability contributes to the assessment of the cumulative impacts of public and private actions and failures to act, and helps capture some of the externalities ignored or inaccurately valued by market mechanisms. These mechanisms include lending and investment policies, risk/reward assessments, and consumer, business, and government purchasing decisions.

As the interest in livability continues to grow, there is increasing concern about the influence of transportation systems on the environment, economic health, and social well-being at geographic scales ranging from the local to the national. The Internet has changed the way data are developed, packaged, integrated, and used in decision making. During the past decade, Americans have witnessed a proliferation of local, state, and even national livability plans and agendas. Examples at these scales include Miami-Dade, Florida's, 79th Street Corridor revitalization; California's Smart Investment plan; and the Clinton-Gore administration's Livable Communities Initiative (U.S. White House Task Force on Livable Communities, 2000). Moreover, innovative public policy initiatives such as location-efficient mortgages, taxation schemes to constrain urban sprawl, and pollution credit trading rely on livability concepts and measures. In addition, many private firms are using livability information in their decisions about facility siting, employment creation, insurance, and marketing.

Why has the concept of livability, especially for America's cities and suburbs, suddenly become so important? This is a complex question. Part of the push toward more livable communities is related to concerns for social well-being, another composite concept (Smith, 1973).

Often, levels of social well-being are a function of the distribution, rather than the allocation, of economic resources. Thus, even if aggregate indicators of economic growth are strong, the qualitative dimensions of the economy are crucial in shaping quality of life and making cities more livable. Dimensions of employment include hours worked (full-time, part-time, etc.), wage rate, health insurance and retirement benefits, proximity to affordable transit and child care options, and work safety provisions. These aspects of employment contribute to (or detract from) social well-being. In turn, working conditions shape individuals' and families' ability to secure decent housing and pay taxes to support adequate urban services and infrastructure, which translate into variations in community livability.

As disparities in livability grow, those who are able to move out of the worst places and secure better residential environments do so, with much of the dispersal facilitated by regional transportation system investments, including highways and public transportation. This fuels a downward spiral of poverty and reduced livability in the communities they leave behind. At a more philosophical level, the social contract, and the norms for social equity and fairness that it implies, are central to one's subjective, collective sense of well-being. Thus, large disparities in the livability of cities and suburbs generate deep dissatisfaction, underlie episodes of social unrest and dysfunction, and reduce the quality of life for all.

Part of this dynamic is clearly rooted in the economy. During recessions, concerns for livability arise as cities, suburbs, and towns compete for a larger share of a shrinking economic pie, by making themselves attractive to prospective employers and workers. They also seek to retain existing firms and residents. As the economy rebounds (as it did during the late 1990s), rapid growth typically generates additional traffic congestion, housing price escalation, rising consumption of goods and services (and attendant waste), and the loss of farmland and natural areas to suburban and exurban expansion. The resulting threats to the quality of everyday residential environments lead to political pressure to contain or at least shape growth in ways that promote the continued livability of the community.

At another level of economic concern, livability has become vital as cities and regions are increasingly expected to compete for economic activity with other nations and metropolitan regions throughout the world (Scott, 1998). Economic globalization and the increasing mobility of both populations and capital have eroded the autonomy of nation-states and their ability to direct growth and have also left major concentrations of economic activity—city-regions, or what Pierce and colleagues (1993) term "citistates"—to fend for themselves in a global marketplace. Globalization may create a host of livability challenges for localities as it drives demographic change, economic restructuring, and provision of urban services (see NRC, 1999). In this marketplace, employers, tourists, business travelers, and (to a lesser extent) workers themselves enjoy an enormous range of choice. It only stands to reason that the places that are more livable and have distinctive identities will have a competitive edge. Hence, one local response is to push for greater livability to facilitate the "selling" of places (Kearns and Philo, 1993).

Finally, and importantly, concerns for livability are also rooted in an increasing recognition that current patterns of urban life and consumption habits are neither healthy nor sustainable over the longer term and that our environment has a finite supply of resources with which to support the world's population. New biomedical research reveals an ever-growing prevalence of pollution-linked health problems, along with the recognition that urban regions are often hotspots for water, air, and soil pollution resulting from their long histories of unregulated heavy industrialization and reliance on the automobile (see NRC, 1988). In addition, major cities of the developed world consume a disproportionate share of ecosystem resources such as water, forest, and aquatic ecosystem resources, as well as waste assimilation capacity.

Central for many urban residents, especially communities made up of minorities, is a measure of environmental justice to ensure that no one segment of the population either suffers from disproportionate exposure to environmental hazards or is denied access to environmental amenities such as urban open space. For many, increasing livability is closely linked to reducing what Wackernagel and Rees (1996) term our ecological "footprint," and to efforts to prevent pollution and reduce waste, conserve natural resources and wildlife habitat, and protect endangered species (see Box 1.1).

In sum, livability is complex multifaceted concept. It is also a highly relative term: what would be considered a livable community in one part of the world might be deemed highly unsatisfactory in another. This might be due to cultural differences or to different standards of living that alter expectations for urban design, transportation, other infrastructure, and service provision. Nevertheless, the idea of livability remains a powerful one. In fact, it is the very generality of the term that allows diverse groups of stakeholders to come together and make livability a public policy goal.

BOX 1.1
Ecological Footprint

A good example of a complex crosscutting measure is the ecological footprint, a measure of the amount of biologically productive land and water required to produce the resources consumed and to assimilate the wastes generated by an individual, company, community, or country. This measure can be used at various spatial scales, and by analyzing consumption patterns (including an accounting of where goods consumed come from, how much it costs in natural resource terms to import them, where waste is deposited, etc.) it can illustrate how a particular place appropriates resources both from its own hinterlands and from "distant elsewheres" around the globe—a feature increasingly vital under conditions of rapid globalization that are progressively detaching the impacts of consumption decisions from the location of consumption.

SOURCE: Wackernagel and Rees (1996).

Indicators of Livability

At the local level, communities are working to develop more attractive and functional shopping and business centers, build affordable housing, promote transit utilization and transit-supportive land use, and protect open space. In some cases, these efforts focus on a specific facility and amenity; in other instances, the agenda is broader. In each of these cases, livability must be defined in some way that allows components or indicators of livability for that particular community to be identified and assessed.

Some cities (e.g., Santa Monica, California) have launched "sustainable cities" programs, designed to promote the creation of high-quality jobs, affordable housing units, and environmental quality, while reducing energy use and toxic emissions. Often these plans represent a cooperative effort on the part of the public and private sectors to reach shared goals. In Moline, Illinois, for example, a public-private partnership, Renew Moline, was created to attract business to the decaying downtown riverfront and to develop a major new waterfront "commons" to draw jobs and visitors downtown. In Tucson, Arizona, the city and its private and public sector partners built a large-scale, pedestrian-oriented, mixed-use development whose homes use half the energy consumed by the typical Tucson area house (U.S. White House Task Force on Livable Communities, 2000).

Larger regions are also launching programs to improve livability; in the Salt Lake City metropolitan area, Envision Utah mounted a large-scale participatory effort to plan for future livability (see Box 1.2; http://www.envisionutah.org), while Sustainable Seattle has created a set of indicators designed to track the region's performance on a variety of livability dimensions (http://www.scn.org/sustainable/susthome.html). States are also promoting such efforts; for example, Maryland is directing state infrastructure investments to already developed urban areas in order to increase well-being in disadvantaged neighborhoods and to conserve farmland and wild areas (U.S. White House Task Force on Livable Communities, 2000).

BOX 1.2
Case Study on Envision Utah

The urbanized area of northern Utah is experiencing tremendous growth. The Greater Wasatch Area (GWA), including the region from Nephi to Brigham City and from Kamas to Grantsville, consists of 88 cities and towns, and spans 10 counties. The GWA has 1.7 million residents, which is expected to increase to 2.7 million by 2020 and 5 million by 2050. The region's developable private land is surrounded by mountains, lakes, and public lands, which create a natural growth boundary. Dramatic increases in population and land consumption will impact the quality of life and costs of living in this area. Air quality will suffer, new water sources will have to be developed, and crowding and congestion will increase. Housing costs will increase as land becomes scarcer, crime will increase, business and personal costs will increase, and government spending on infrastructure will increase.

Envision Utah was formed in January of 1997 to address these concerns. Envision Utah is a public-private community partnership dedicated to studying the effects of long-term growth in the Greater Wasatch Area. The Envision Utah partnership includes state and local government officials, business leaders, developers, conservationists, landowners, academicians, church and community groups, and general citizens. Sponsored by the Coalition for Utah's Future, Envision Utah and its partners, together with the public, have developed a publicly supported growth strategy that will preserve Utah's high quality of life, natural environment, and economic vitality during the next 50 years. Envision Utah was established to develop a broadly supported growth strategy, a common vision for the future to guide residents, businesses, and government bodies of Utah well into the twenty-first century. Envision Utah is a unique and dynamic partnership, bringing together citizens, business leaders, and policy makers from public and private circles throughout the state.

This unique and diverse coalition is working to implement a common vision for the Greater Wasatch Area. This group did not seek to limit growth, but rather to create a vision of how the citizens of GWA want the area to grow. Envision Utah incorporated substantial input from the public. Meetings, surveys, and open work-

continued

Box 1.2 Continued

shops have been held throughout the region and will continue to occur as Envision Utah works toward implementation of the Quality Growth Strategy. This effort has involved over 175 public meetings, with more than 6,000 participants, the distribution of 800,000 questionnaires across the region, more than 70,000 work hours dedicated to technical modeling, and scores of meetings with key decision makers—all designed to help chart the course for future development. The ideas and opinions contributed to this process will be key to successful implementation.

The first phase of the Envision Utah process included an in-depth study conducted to determine Utahans' values and to find out what they most want to preserve or change as Utah continues to grow. Following the study, a baseline model was generated with extensive computer analysis (Quality Growth Efficiency Tools, QGET) by the Governor's Office of Planning and Budget, to project the effects of growth during the next 20 to 50 years based on current trends. A series of public workshops were held to gather public opinion and data from GWA citizens, which included extensive work on regional maps and exploration of important topics such as land use, transportation, and open space preservation. The public input was valuable and key in the development of alternative growth scenarios.

Four alternative growth scenarios were developed to show possible patterns that could result from various growth strategies implemented during the next 20 to 50 years. The alternatives ranged from a very auto-oriented, spread-out development, to significant increases in densities and extensive transit systems. An analysis of these alternative scenarios was conducted to determine the relative costs and impacts of each strategy on population, infrastructure costs, air quality, water, open space and recreation preservation, traffic congestion, affordable housing, business patterns, and other significant variables. A widespread campaign was launched to encourage area residents to express their preferences for future development and to increase understanding of the options and challenges inherent in growth. A public survey was conducted and workshops were held to garner citizens' input regarding the specific growth scenario they wanted to pursue. A compilation and analysis of this input was used to determine the primary goals for the draft Quality Growth Strategy. In addition, a housing analysis to the year 2020 was conducted to help gauge the housing needs and wants of current and future GWA residents.

The Quality Growth Strategy identified six primary goals including (1) enhancing air quality; (2) increasing mobility and transportation choices; (3) preserving critical lands; (4) conserving and maintaining availability of water resources; (5) providing housing opportunities for a range of family and income types; and (6) maximizing efficiency in public infrastructure investments to promote the other goals. These goals are supported by 32 key strategies, some of which are listed below. These strategies were developed by working with key stakeholders and the residents of the community to provide realistic ideas for the Greater Wasatch Area to implement the goals developed in the Quality Growth Strategy. The strategies utilized market-based approaches such as state and local incentives and sought to effect change through education and promotion, rather than regulatory means. The strategies that they employed included the following:

continued

Box 1.2 Continued

- promoting walkable development by encouraging new and existing developments to include a mix of uses with pedestrian-friendly design;
- promoting the development of a region-wide transit system that could utilize buses, bus ways, light rail, lower-cost self-powered rail technology, commuter rail, and small buses to make transit more effective and convenient;
- promoting the development of a network of bikeways and trails for recreation and commuting;
- fostering transit-oriented development such as housing and commercial developments that incorporate and encourage various forms of public transportation;
- preserving open lands by encouraging developments that include open areas and providing incentives for the reuse of currently developed lands;
- restructuring water bills to encourage water conservation;
- fostering mixed-use, mixed-income, walkable neighborhoods to provide a greater array of housing choices.

Envision Utah's objective was to analyze and disseminate information on the costs and benefits associated with these strategies and to work with local and state governments, citizens, developers, conservationists, civic groups, and others. With the Quality Growth Strategy in hand, Envision Utah must now work to ensure that it is the guiding tool for future development in the Greater Wasatch Area.

Over the past year, Envision Utah has developed Utah-specific urban planning tools to help decision makers implement the Quality Growth Strategy. Envision Utah has trained more than 1,000 local officials, planners, developers, realtors, and other key stakeholders to help them use these tools in the most effective manner. In addition, Quality Growth Demonstration Projects are currently under way in three sub-regions to develop regional plans for each area that will help facilitate substantial change in local policies to help implement quality growth principles. Envision Utah's strategies have provided community leaders with the information to broaden the choices available and to facilitate more informed decision making.

Envision Utah will continue to educate decision makers concerning quality growth strategies at all appropriate levels of government, to help maintain and build support for action. Intergovernmental and interlocal agreements, local zoning and planning decision making, state incentives for communities implementing the Quality Growth Strategy, and legislative action to promote quality growth are the ultimate goals of Envision Utah.

SOURCES:
Envision Utah, Envision Utah Quality Growth Strategy, (November 1999);
Envision Utah web site, Coalition for Utah's Future, http://www.envisionutah.org/ Accessed July 1, 2001;
Quality Growth Efficiency Tools Technical Committee, Baseline Scenario, February 1998;
Quality Growth Efficiency Tools Technical Committee, Scenario Analysis, March 1999;
Quality Growth Efficiency Tools Technical Committee, Strategy Analysis, May 2000.
Envision Utah Toolbox, Urban Planning Tools for Quality Growth; First edition and 2002 supplement.

A problem closely related to loss of wildlands and open space is species endangerment. In the United States, urbanization poses a greater threat to species than any other single phenomenon. Transportation supports urbanization, agricultural development, and other industrial activities that are strongly associated with habitat loss and species endangerment. There are nearly 4 million miles of roadway in the United States, and this system is accompanied by railroad track, pipeline, and other infrastructure and facilities that occupy large amounts of land, modify the local environment, and create ecological effects over broad geographic areas (NRC, 1997). Of the 877 U.S. species listed as threatened or endangered in 1994, 94 were endangered directly by road presence, construction, and maintenance (Czech et al., 2000).

When the geographical distribution of species endangerment is analyzed, in all sectors, "hotspots" are identified (Dobson et al., 1997) that coincide with areas of economic growth. For example, these hotspots appear in southern Florida, California, and east-central Texas. In their supporting role for economic development in all sectors, transportation decisions significantly impact the natural environment. Transportation decisions have a far reaching impact on systems such as CO_2 and NO_x levels in the atmosphere as a result of emissions, water flow in watersheds, and impediments to the physical movement of species including feeding, breeding, and dispersal patterns (NRC, 1997).

Whereas in the United States, livability- and sustainability-oriented plans often tend to be grassroots-initiated efforts mounted in response to local and regional problems (Farrell and Hart, 1998), other regions of the world have placed more emphasis on national or even larger-scale efforts. Local Agenda 21, for example, which grew out of the Rio Earth Summit in 1992, launched many such efforts, especially in Europe and the developing world, many of which address livability issues. For example, as of the late 1990s, more that 1,000 European localities had undertaken some form of Local Agenda 21 projects, many of them involving livability/ sustainability indicators (Beatley, 2000, pp. 22, 422). Localities in Asia had 300 such efforts by 1998 (ICLEI, 1999). In the United States, communities that initiated local Agenda 21 programs tended to be in areas experiencing rapid economic growth where severe strains were imposed on environmental and cultural resources (Lake, 2000).

Increasingly, nonprofit organizations, whether working alone or in partnership with government agencies, have used such indicators to develop local, national, and regional campaigns. Leicester, U.K., for instance, designed a set of 14 measures in the mid-1990s to track sustainability and provide a way for the city to measure how well or poorly it is doing, as well as indicators for advocacy around key environmental problems. Other cities, including Amsterdam and Den Haag, in The Netherlands;

Freiburg, Germany; and Leicester, U.K., collaborated to create the European Sustainability Index Project, creating 26 different indicators (Lake, 2000, p. 328).

Hart (1999) provides a comprehensive overview of sustainable community indicators. Genres of local indicators include transportation (infrastructure, commuting, public transit, and vehicles, in addition to the number of pedestrian-friendly streets, ratio of bike paths to streets, percentage of street miles designated bike route miles); ecosystem integrity (biodiversity, fish, land use, soil, surface water, and wetlands); community involvement (volunteerism and connectedness, [e.g., number of community gardens, and distances between residences of extended family members]); and equity (diversity, employment types, income, children, finance). Attention to the interrelationships among these types of indicators is key.

KEY DIMENSIONS OF LIVABILITY

Livability depends upon three key, interdependent spheres of social life: the economy, social well-being, and the environment. The economy, which supplies jobs and income, is fundamental to residents' health (e.g., their ability to obtain food, clothing, and shelter), as well as higher-order needs such as education, health care, and recreation. At the same time, the economy should efficiently utilize raw materials drawn from the environment, so as to ensure sufficient resources for current and future generations. Social well-being relies, in large part, on justice: a social and spatial distribution of economic and environmental resources that is fair, as well as systems of governance that are inclusive of all residents. Individual freedom and opportunity are also important components and precursors of social well-being.

The environment is the critical infrastructure that provides natural resources, the capacity for waste assimilation, and links between people and the natural world. If adequate functioning ceases within any of these three spheres, human settlements can quickly deteriorate, resulting in population loss, poverty, social conflict, and elevated levels of environmental health problems. This fundamental "golden triad" of livability is often portrayed by one of four schematics displayed in Figures 1.1 through 1.4.

The "golden triad" embraces widely shared goals—economic efficiency, social justice, and environmental protection. As discussed in more detail below, such goals are often treated independently and are entirely separable (Figure 1.1). Alternatively, they are viewed as equally important and capable of being balanced without undue conflict (Figure 1.2) in order to achieve health, justice, and efficient communities. This is, per-

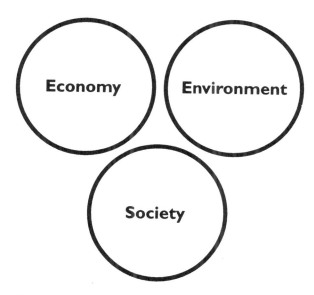

FIGURE 1.1 Community as three separate spheres. SOURCE: Hart (1999).

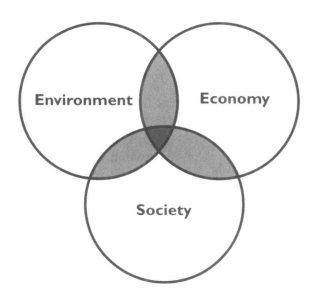

FIGURE 1.2 Community as three interconnected spheres. SOURCE: Hart (1999).

haps, the most common approach to livability dimensions, with the interactions more explicitly spelled out and the central goal—livability—occupying center stage.

Both perspectives gloss over conflicts among goals associated with the three spheres, and neither suggests the complexity of interactions among spheres. Only Figure 1.3 recognizes the fact that the environment is, inescapably, the critical infrastructure without which neither an economy nor a society can survive. Only Figure 1.4, while representing the three basic spheres, emphasizes the web-like nature of relations between the economy, environment, and society.

Despite various conceptual underpinnings, ideas and indicators of livability do influence decision making on a variety of important fronts. There are numerous examples, ranging from transit-oriented urban developments, to local "smart growth" and sustainability plans, to state programs that redirect investment to neglected urban areas, all the way to the federal government's Livable Communities Initiative, a package of policy initiatives and partnerships developed by the U.S. White House Task Force on Livable Communities (2000).

LIVABILITY AND INDICATORS

How, exactly, are broad ideas about livability translated into a set of practical guidelines for policy making? In general, the key dimensions of livability tend to be converted to a much more specific set of indicators that can be used for evaluation. Indicators have long been used by planners, policy makers, and public managers to profile populations and com-

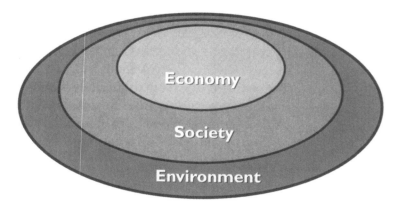

FIGURE 1.3 Community as three integrated spheres. SOURCE: Hart (1999).

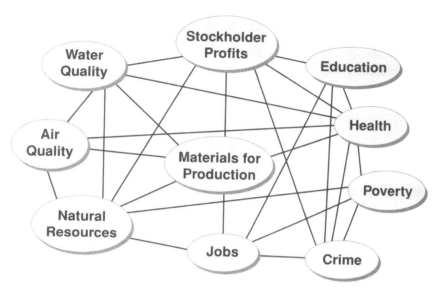

FIGURE 1.4 Community as a web of relations among spheres. SOURCE: Hart (1999).

munities and to track economic, social, and environmental changes (Knox, 1975). They also have been harnessed to measure and track livability. Sometimes, available sets of livability indicators, such as the U.S. Department of Agriculture's "Natural Amenities" index for counties (which measures topography, climate, and other physical features of places), are of questionable value for planning because chosen indicators are not susceptible to policy-induced change. There are also commercially oriented ratings of urban places that have been produced for some time, based on a limited number of key place-specific variables (for instance, the popular "Places Rated" series and *Money* magazine's ratings). However, most of these are of questionable value for analysis and planning purposes (Henderson, 1997).

The fundamental spheres of livability are typically reflected by specific indices, much as our national economy is tracked through the use of measures such as Gross Domestic Product (GDP). At the urban level, for example, traditional indices include those listed in Table 1.1.

Increasingly, however, new indicators that reflect the web-like interactions portrayed in Figure 1.4, are being utilized. These indicators emphasize the interconnectedness of people and places, rather than traditional "silo" or stovepipe-type thinking about the economy, society, and

TABLE 1.1 Traditional Place-Based Indicators

Economic	Social	Environmental
Median income	Percentage of registered voters	Ambient air quality
Unemployment rate	High school graduation rate	Water quality
Job growth rate	Poverty rate	Open space per capita
Gross regional product	Infant mortality rate	Incidence of pollution-related illness

environment. An example of such new indicators, adapted from Hart (1999), appears in Table 1.2.

In addition, very different types of indicators have been developed that are even more challenging to traditional ways of thinking about livability and progress. Concepts such as "natural capital" and "nature's services," as well as ideas about "cultural resources," have been used to propose alternatives to traditional types of indicators. Some are becoming familiar, for instance, the Genuine Progress Indicator proposed as a substitute for GDP, which considers not only factors such as job creation, but also nontraditional factors—for example, the amount of workers' discretionary time—or a more complex measure, such as the proportion of job growth that is linked to remediation of problems created by the economy (environmental cleanup, health care issues, or the employment impacts of a major natural disaster) versus job expansion that reflects positive development in economic capacity. Other indicators are more speculative but gaining some acceptance; for example, ideas of natural capital that translate into measures of economic activity consider the extent to which certain forms of industrial activity deplete key stores of natural resources, rather than considering only the creation of jobs or financial wealth. The ecological footprint described in Box 1.1 represents such a crosscutting measure. These indicators are expressed in units such as "miles of salmon run degraded per kilowatt of hydroelectrical energy produced and consumed per new job created by the aluminum sector." Similarly, the recognition that cultural or social capital is vital to the proper functioning and livability of communities translates into indicators such as "voluntary associates per capita" or "per capita hours of participation in community-based activities." Other emerging types of indicators are linked to notions of nature or ecosystem services—namely, the real work that the air, water, and soil do to keep the ambient environment clean and functioning as our

TABLE 1.2 New-Generation Livability Indicators

Economic	Social	Environmental
Hours of paid work at the living wage	Students trained for local jobs	Use of toxic materials in economy
Diversity of job base	Voting rate	Vehicle-miles traveled
Wages paid and spent locally	Percentage covered by health insurance	Percentage of recyclable products used
Percentage of local economy based on renewable resources	Welfare-to-workers above poverty	Ratio of renewable to nonrenewable energy

environmental support system. These indicators lead away from standard measures, such as "road miles per capita" toward measures such as "loss of stormwater absorption capacity per road mile constructed."

In transportation planning, traditional system indicators, such as pedestrian volume or mean commute time, have been used more often than livability indicators. Traditional transportation measures focus on the performance of the transportation system, rather than on the economic, social, and environmental impacts of such systems on aspects of places and everyday life. Traditional indicators tend to ignore the conditions imposed on communities through which the transportation system passes and the impacts of transportation decisions on energy consumption. They may also, for example, incorrectly equate mobility with access, when in fact access is a more complex issue that is related to equity and availability of resources (Knox, 1982). Indeed, there is no definitive or commonly accepted set of livability indicators related to transportation, suggesting that indicator research and development for transportation-livability planning could be a useful and rewarding endeavor. An example of a transportation-livability program included in Box 1.3 demonstrates the economic value of compact communities with access to public transportation.

How might a relatively traditional set of transportation planning-based indicators compare to one premised on notions of livability? The ideas behind these approaches are distinct. Traditional measures emphasize the economic role of transportation systems, given their importance to goods movement, consumer access, and worker mobility, and the economic costs of inefficient transport services (due to delays, injury, etc.). Livability-based measures are concerned not only with how efficient the

BOX 1.3
Fannie Mae Location Efficient Mortgage

In 1998, Fannie Mae agreed to a $100 million demonstration of the Location Efficient Mortgage (LEM) in several major cities, including Chicago. This initiative is an example of a private effort that promotes and fosters livable communities. This loan is designed to help people buy homes in neighborhoods where they can "live locally," that is, rely on public transportation to work, shop, attend school, and carry out other activities of daily life. Research conducted by the Center for Neighborhood Technology, the Natural Resources Defense Council, and the Surface Transportation Policy Project showed that in Chicago, Los Angeles, and San Francisco, residents located in compact neighborhoods or traditional suburban areas with excellent public transportation services traveled less than half the average vehicle-miles than those who lived in sprawling suburban or exurban areas.

A carefully researched computer model was built that can predict how many miles are driven and how many cars would be owned by an average household in each part of a metropolitan area, based on location. The difference between urban and suburban car ownership and use was clear. Location efficiency is used to describe some of the urban households that devote substantially less of their income to meet their day-to-day transportation needs. LEM borrowers must prefer to live in a compact urban neighborhood; make many trips by foot, bicycle, or public transportation; and rely on locally available shopping. Approximately one-fourth of the total number of trips taken each month is job related. The majority of travel includes visits to friends and relatives, going to school or recreational facilities, running errands, shopping, or visiting a place of worship. Therefore, many aspects of the homeowner's life must be conducive to the location efficient lifestyle.

People seeking homes in urban neighborhoods can now obtain a LEM to redirect a significant portion of their budgets from transportation to homeownership. The LEM borrower could be expected to manage a mortgage that is $15,000 to $50,000 more than other mortgage products. The benefits of LEM include the following:

- increasing the buying power of low- to mid-income homeowners,
- increasing the home purchases in a variety of urban communities,
- increasing public transit ridership,
- supporting local consumer services and cultural amenities,
- reducing energy consumption,
- improving local and regional air quality, and
- promoting the development and maintenance of livable communities.

SOURCE: Fannie Mae (1999).

transportation system is, but also with the impact of all modes of transportation on the everyday life and health of residents and with the implications of transportation for the environment, especially land use, energy and materials consumption, and pollution. Such measures are increasingly being used; crosscutting measures in Table 1.2 are drawn from community livability, sustainability, or healthy city plans created by federal agencies such as the Environmental Protection Agency, state planning agencies, city governments, community councils, county health departments, and nonprofit organizations from both the United States and Canada.

An example of such a transportation-related livability measure is Pedestrian Friendly Streets (Hart, 1998a) used by the City of Richmond in British Columbia as well as by Sustainable Seattle. This indicator measured the length and proportion of major streets that met the city's minimum standard: a sidewalk on one or both sides of the street. In addition, it measured streets that met a higher standard where the street and sidewalk were separated by a tree-lined median or parking row to cut noise and increase safety for pedestrians.

When the City of Richmond began tracking this indicator in 1990, many of its streets did not meet the official minimum standard, and none met the higher standard. However, by the late 1990s, after the indicator had called attention to this issue, a majority of streets had been improved to meet the minimum standard, and one-fifth of the streets actually met the higher standard. This sort of indicator, which addresses the extent to which the city's transportation infrastructure encourages walking, speaks simultaneously to economic, social, and environmental concerns: more pedestrian traffic on major commercial streets stimulates retail activity, encourages social interaction and exercise, reduces risk of traffic accidents, and can reduce automobile use and thus air pollution emissions. This indicator could also be usefully elaborated by considering the extent to which pedestrian-friendly streets actually link neighborhoods to commercial districts.

This example serves to illustrate the importance of indicator selection. The choice of indicators is critical to enabling community members, planners, and decision makers to focus on the desired outcomes of transportation, land use, and economic development decisions and then to measure the attributes of livability that result from their actions.

At a broader regional scale, in Charlottesville, Virginia, the Thomas Jefferson Sustainability Council has created a set of livability indicators for the Thomas Jefferson District Planning Council, the region's council of government (Box 1.4). Part of a broader indicators program, their transportation indicators are linked to critical goals and to a series of innovative indicators similar to those in Table 1.2. All of these indicators reflect livability concerns.

Given a goal of facilitating the circulation of people, goods, services and information through integrated systems that minimize adverse im-

BOX 1.4
Thomas Jefferson Area Eastern Planning Initiative

The Thomas Jefferson Planning district near Charlottesville, Virginia, established the Eastern Planning Initiative (EPI) and set the following goals that it wanted to address in an integrated manner:

- to develop an interactive land use / transportation computer model (ComPlan);
- to create a 50-year vision and implementation strategy for the area; and
- to develop a handbook and a model for other communities.

EPI's plan included identifying existing community elements, creating ideal community elements, and launching a demonstration computer model so that stakeholders could envision alternative futures. It wanted to develop land use/transportation scenarios that allowed the public to evaluate alternatives and select the most desirable scenarios.

The project team included an advisory committee, the Planning District Commission, Virginia Department of Transportation, Virginia Department of Rail and Public Transportation, Federal Highway Administration, local planners, the University of Virginia School of Architecture and Design Center at the Institute for Sustainable Design, and the Renaissance Team.

The first step was to create a 50-year vision. This included establishing a regional plan, community elements, and an implementation plan. The regional plan considered distribution and density of people and jobs. In an effort to determine where people would live, the project team established a regional framework that integrated environmental features and infrastructure and included several alternative futures and visions. Three questions were identified: What types of communities should be considered? Where are the different communities located? How are these communities connected?

To address these questions, the team considered a variety of community variables (elements). Data that were to define the existing community elements included evaluations of open space, building proximity, building scale, street scale, street character, internal paths, external connectivity, parking, and other types of activity in the area. Urban land use elements included residential, mixed use, university/institution, and parks/recreation. Suburban elements included residential, mixed use, retail, office, institutional, industrial, parks/recreation, and conservation areas. Rural land usage included small town, village, residential, mixed use, industrial, parks/recreation, agricultural/forestal, and conservation areas.

The definition of mixed use varied with development densities. In an urban area, mixed use is typically a densely developed or densely populated area or a community within a metropolitan context containing more than one of the following land uses: residential, retail, office, civic, institutional, or industrial. Suburban mixed use refers to an edge community, suburban neighborhood or community, or suburban power center that contains one or more of the following land uses: residential, retail, office, industrial, or institutional. Rural mixed-use areas are sparsely developed or sparsely populated areas with a community that contains more than one of the fol-

continued

(A) Photograph of urban mixed use on East Market Street, Charlottesville, Virginia. SOURCE: Kenneth Schwartz, University of Virginia, Charlottesville.

(B) Photograph of suburban mixed use, Forest Lakes planned community in Albemarle County, Virginia. SOURCE: Kenneth Schwartz, University of Virginia, Charlottesville.

(C) Photograph of rural mixed use, Zion Crossroads, Virginia. SOURCE: Kenneth Schwartz, University of Virginia, Charlottesville.

continued

Box 1.4 Continued

lowing land uses: residential, retail, office, industrial, institutional, and agricultural/forest. The major element distinctions in the different development density areas include open space, different activities, internal path connectivity, building proximity, and parking.

In recognizing these distinctions, EPI planned on enhancing different types of land use for the different types of communities. The vision promoted development of university and institution space in urban areas, suburban mixed-use, retail, office and residential development, and rural residential development. EPI built community consensus through meetings, community workshops, focus groups, newsletters / fact sheets, and a web site. The CorPlan Model was then established to link land use plans and transportation choices. The first step in developing this model was establishing an open space inventory on a GIS base map. Development-prohibited land was marked. Open spaces were categorized as environmentally sensitive, historically significant, agriculture / forest view-sheds, or possible greenway linking systems. (See the community element diagrams in Plates 1 and 2.)

These maps were used to evaluate a variety of future scenarios based on alternate mapping of dispersed, nodal, and urban core development. Next, social factors were included in the analysis. EPI compared different communities by population and employment. Goals were developed by considering personal, community, and regional perspectives and scenario evaluations on these issues. The sustainability council considered quality-of-life goals such as health, urban/suburban relationships, optimal population size, distribution of biological diversity, and water quality and quantity. This effort sought to strike a balance between built areas and open space. Other goals included human-scale development, healthy farms and forests, transportation choices, energy conservation, access to education, access to employment, active citizen participation and a sense of community, and historic preservation.

SOURCE: Bowerman et al. (1996).

---

pacts on natural systems and communities, some of the key objectives and indicators can be viewed in Table 1.3.

In sum, a wide variety of indicators have been proposed and used to assess the livability of places, at varying geographic scales. Traditional transportation indicators are clearly most useful for relatively narrow transportation system investment, improvement, and management decisions; transportation-related livability indicators, in contrast, have more general applicability to the quality of life in a place as it relates to transportation infrastructure and utilization patterns (Box 1.5). Increasingly, such indicators are being incorporated into livability studies by localities, metropolitan regions, and state-level planning efforts.

TABLE 1.3 List of Community Objectives and Associated Indicators

Objective	Indicator
Construct a network of bicycle and pedestrian facilities within urban areas in accordance with the localities' bicycle plans	Linear miles of facilities constructed especially for pedestrian and bicycle use
Connect urban areas of the cities and counties with bikeways and walkways	Linear miles of facilities constructed especially for pedestrian and bicycle use
Reduce automobile and truck traffic volume and speed in residential areas for the safety of children bicycling and playing in these places	Linear miles of traffic-calmed roads
Measure costs of traffic congestion to initiate planning for transit systems	Automobile travel time for series of key automobile transportation system segments

Indicators in Practice

Before livability indicators can begin to play a more significant role in transportation and other areas of decision making, it is necessary to understand basic issues surrounding indicators and their use. In reviewing the history of indicator use, analysts increasingly recognize that the use of indicators is often problematic (Cobb and Rixford, 1998). Neither standard livability indicator sets nor the more elaborate places-rated approaches that include many variables are adequate to capture the many critical dimensions of urban livability (Landis and Sawicki, 1998). Major problems of standard indicators are listed in Table 1.4, and several of these problems are discussed below. Although some are inescapable, regardless of the type or formulation of the indicator used (such as scale), many can be addressed through the use of a new generation of indicators that, for example, explicitly attempt to span dimensions of livability. Also, using indicators in a more sophisticated fashion, and acknowledging their ambiguity and political ramifications, rather than assuming that seemingly simple indicators unambiguously measure major aspects of livability, can skirt pitfalls of indicator use. (For further discussion see Bauer, 1966; U.S. Department of Health, Education and Welfare, 1969; OMB, 1973; Andrews and Withey, c. 1976; Campbell et al., c. 1976.)

BOX 1.5
Livability Versus Transportation Indicators

Traditional Measures
- Patterns of transportation investments by mode
- Flows of people, information, goods, and services
- Capacity of transportation facilities
- Pedestrian volumes
- Percentage of population within 50 miles of air passenger service
- Number of transfers on transit
- Reliability of transit
- Auto-commute and rail accidents
- Mean commute time
- Average road speed
- Waiting time at major intersections
- Road congestion and travel times

Crosscutting Measures
- New housing units or businesses within 5 minutes of public transit
- Percentage of population able to walk or bike to work, school, and shopping
- Percentage of streets with pedestrian and bicycle facilities
- Percentage of commuters using public transit
- Percentage of workers within 30 minutes of work
- Transportation system-related noise levels
- Auto emissions per capita
- Ratio of fuel-efficient to inefficient vehicles
- Ratio of renewably fueled to non-renewably fueled vehicles
- Ratio of highway to transit expenditures
- Percentage of land allocated to automobile use and storage
- Change in total and per-person vehicle-miles traveled

SOURCE: Hart (1998b, 1999).

Appropriate Scale of Analysis

At what scale should livability be measured? Can or should it be considered at the individual, household, or population group scale or only with reference to places? We can improve livability for people, for example, by augmenting their disposable income and thereby allowing them to leave a deteriorating neighborhood. Conversely, it is possible to increase a community's livability without helping any of its original residents who may in fact be displaced as the neighborhood improves and

TABLE 1.4 Lessons of History About Indicator Selection for Practitioners Today

Lessons of History for Practitioners Today	
1. Having a number does not necessarily mean that you have a good indicator	Indicators are quantities to infer qualities. Many believe that if an official agency has measured something, an indicator based on that measure is likely to be valuable. However, quality is elusive, and trying to measure it with a single number often gives misleading results.
2. Effective indicators require a clear conceptual basis	To create a good indicator, you need to clarify exactly what you are trying to measure. Taking time to develop conceptual clarity before gathering data is necessary so that the numbers generated can be deciphered. Careless definitions can lead to inaccurate statistics or bad policies.
3. There is no such thing as a value-free indicator	The act of deciding what to count and not to count requires value judgments. Indicators carry implicit messages. There are complex methods to deal with bias in survey questions, but some matters are too sensitive.
4. Comprehensiveness may be the enemy of effectiveness	Historically, the most powerful indicator studies have focused on a single issue. It is most effective to find a few insightful and compelling indicators to represent a complex whole.
5. The symbolic value of an indicator may outweigh its value as a literal measure	Numbers can act as metaphors, which is especially true of index numbers. For example, the Genuine Progress Indicator (GPI) is not a literal measure of well-being, but rather a metaphor for progress.
6. Don't conflate indicators with reality	Every indicator is a flawed representation of a complex set of events and, at best, a fractional measurement of reality. Researchers should strive to develop multiple indicators for the same phenomenon so that the resulting numbers do not become a barrier to the truth.
7. A democratic indicators program requires more than good public participation processes	Widespread participation may not be the best "indicator" of whether an indicator project is really democratic. Procedural justice will not automatically bring about substantive justice. Social reports often have a political edge when not striving for consensus.
8. Measurement does not necessarily induce appropriate action	New information contained in indicators may change perceptions, but the connections to actions are not automatic. In addition, action sometimes precedes the development of indicators.

continued

TABLE 1.4 Continued

9. Better information may lead to better decisions and improved outcomes, but not as easily as it might seem	The policy-making function of indicators is indirect. Better statistics will not always lead to better decisions. The information has to affect motives or perceptions of how the world works.
10. Challenging prevailing wisdom about what causes a problem is often the first step to fixing it	Drawing attention to a previously ignored condition, finding a new connection between two factors, or showing that a widely shared idea is wrong can lead to convincing analysis of why a problem exists, so that a new solution can be adopted.
11. To take action, look for indicators that reveal causes, not symptoms	In order to alter a symptom, it is necessary to have a theory about what is causing it.
12. You are more likely to move from indicators to outcomes if you have control over resources	The purpose of an indicator is to alert the public and policy makers to problems so that they can be solved. This can occur only when researchers have a connection with those in power. Otherwise, the indicators may not influence outcomes.

SOURCE: Cobb and Rixford (1998).

becomes more attractive to higher-income households. The need to focus on both people and places when planning for livable communities is discussed again in Chapter 2.

Even if a place-based approach is adopted, the question of scale still arises. Indicators of neighborhood livability, for example, cannot always be scaled up to a regional or state level, in the same way that large-scale indicators are not necessarily relevant at the community level. Even if scaling up or down is possible, it might not make sense from a policy perspective. For example, although health indicators such as infant mortality are meaningful at both local and global scales, many transportation or mobility indicators have little relevance at the global scale. A case in point is "walkability," which can be measured only at a local scale and has relevance only up to a regional scale. Similarly, we might be able to take neighborhood air quality measurements crucial for local efforts to remediate a nearby pollution hotspot, but such measures cannot be aggregated to the regional scale where regulatory compliance indicators are crucial for policy making (see NRC, 1999).

distribution of various forms of wealth (i.e., social, natural, or financial capital); measures of ecosystem functioning, such as species richness and protection and habitat protection or augmentation, might serve in an assessment of environmental well-being associated with a livability program.

Politics of Use

Both indicator selection and, especially, benchmarking are profoundly political activities. Indicators themselves can become politicized since their interpretation is often open to question and some have the potential to cast less favorable light than others on specific elements of the community. Thus, selection of a set of livability indicators related to the economy that, for example, focuses on quantitative aspects of economic activity (i.e., rates of job creation and retention, average wages, etc.) may tell a very different story than a set of indicators that includes measures of qualitative growth. Stakeholders are likely to advocate for those indicators that are the most favorable to their interests—either showing them in a positive light or underscoring the need for public investments from which they are likely to benefit.

Because of the politically contentious nature of policy and planning, the launch of a public indicators project may signal political stalemate rather than movement toward the programmatic changes required to make places more livable. The very act of embarking on an indicators effort may reflect the desire among powerful stakeholders to deflect any (potentially undesirable) change in public policy, the expectation being that any large-scale data collection and analysis effort will result in "paralysis by analysis" rather than decisive public action. Livability exercises can become excuses for taking no action and can drag on indefinitely. More cynically, such exercises also may be seen as a "feel-good" way to encourage public involvement and make it seem to occupy center stage, while in fact it is only a means to legitimize decisions being made by key political stakeholders backstage. Such experiences can result in a backlash among resident-participants. Projects initiated by nonprofit organizations, in contrast, may be designed more for advocacy purposes than for use in policy making per se; yet if decision makers systematically ignore group efforts, disillusionment and feelings of disenfranchisement can also result. For all of these reasons, indicators projects can take on a life of their own, effectively divorced from policy and fueled in part by a veritable "indicators industry" consisting of private data vendors, GIS companies, and indicators consultants.

Attempts to set benchmarks are even more likely to produce political conflict than simple indicator-based planning. Since benchmarks, by definition, set targets for local actors—both institutional and individual—they can force the question of how to produce changes in livability and at what cost. The degree of conflict around benchmarks will vary and typically revolves around any enforcement mechanisms (such as sanctions, fines, or rewards) put in place. For example, if there is a 20 percent reduction benchmark for municipal electricity use over a five-year period, someone—agencies, private households, businesses—must determine how to attain this reduction. If there is no consequence for failing to meet the benchmark, then there may be minimal conflict around the 20 percent figure; however, if there are fines or other remedies to compel at least good-faith effort toward meeting the benchmark, then such targets become lightning rods for conflict around livability plans.

REFERENCES

Andrews, C. J. 2001. Analyzing quality-of-place. Environment and Planning B: Planning and Design 23:201-217.

Andrews, Frank M., and Stephen B. Withey. c1976. Social Indicators of Well-Being: Americans' Perceptions of Life Quality. Prepared by the American Academy of Arts and Sciences for the National Aeronautics and Space Administration. New York: Plenum Press. 455 pp.

Bauer, Raymond Augustine, ed. 1966. Social Indicators. Cambridge, Mass.: MIT Press. 357 pp.

Beatley, Timothy. 2000. Green Urbanism: Learning from European Cities. Washington, D.C.: Island Press.

Bowerman, D. P., J. Walker, and M. C. Collins. 1996. Indicators of Sustainability: Interim Report. Available at http://monticello.avenue.gen.va.us/Gov/TJPDC/ind-7'96.html#Accords. Accessed September 25, 2001.

Campbell, Angus, Philip E. Converse, and Willard L. Rodgers. c1976. The Quality of American Life: Perceptions, Evaluations, and Satisfactions. New York: Russell Sage Foundation. 583 pp.

Cobb, Clifford W., and Craig Rixford. 1998. Lessons Learned from the History of Social Indicators. San Francisco: Redefining Progress.

Czech, B., P. R. Krausman, and P. K. Devers. 2000. Economic associations among causes of species endangerment in the United States. BioScience 50(7):593-601.

Dobson, A. P., J. P. Rodriquez, W. M. Roberts, and D. S. Wilcove. 1997. Geographic distribution of endangered species in the Unites States. Science 275:550-553.

Fannie Mae. 1999. Introducing the Location Efficient Home. Available at http://www.locationefficiency.com/lemlifestyle_updated.pdf. Accessed October 7, 2001.

Farrell, Alex, and Maureen Hart. 1998. What does sustainability really mean? The search for useful indicators. Environment 40:4-9.

Franke, Randall. 2000. Quality of life issues will rule. American City and County 115:24-25.

Hart, Maureen. 1998a. Indicator Spotlight: Pedestrian Friendly Streets. Available at http://www.sustainablemeasures.com/Indicators/IS_ Pedestrian.html. Accessed September 25, 2001.

Hart, Maureen. 1998b. Sustainable Measures. Available at www.sustainablemeasures.com. Accessed September 25, 2001.

Hart, Maureen. 1999. Guide to Sustainable Community Indicators, 2nd edition. North Andover, Mass.: Hart Environmental Data.

Henderson, Craig. 1997. Rating livable cities. Public Management 79:23-24.

ICLEI (International Council for Local Environmental Initiatives). 1999. Asia-Pacific Mayors' Action Plan for Sustainable Development and Local Agenda 21. Available at http://www.iclei.org/la21/map_ap.htm. Accessed September 25, 2001.

Kearns, Gerry, and Chris Philo, eds. 1993. Selling Places: The City as Cultural Capital, Past and Present. Oxford, U.K.: Pergamon Press.

Knox, P. L. 1975. Social Well-Being: A Spatial Perspective. Oxford, U.K.: Oxford University Press.

Knox, P. L. 1982. Residential structure, facility location, and patterns of accessibility. In K. Cox and R. J. Johnston, eds., Conflict, Politics, and the Urban Scene. London: Longman.

Knox, P. L., and A. MacLaran. 1978. Values and perceptions in descriptive approaches to urban social geography. In D. Herbert and R. J. Johnston, eds., Geography and the Urban Environment, Vol. 1. Chichester, U.K.: Wiley.

Lake, R. W. 2000. Contradictions at the local scale: Local implementation of Agenda 21 in the USA. Pp. 70-90 in Nicholas Low, Brendan Bleeson, Ingemar Elander, and Rolf Lidskog, eds., Consuming Cities: The Urban Environment in the Global Economy After the Rio Declaration. London: Routledge.

Land, K. 1996. Social indicators and the quality of life: Where do we stand in the mid-1990s? SINET: Social Indicators Network News 45:5-8.

Landis, J. D., and D. S. Sawicki. 1998. A planner's guide to places rated almanac. Journal of the American Planning Association 54:336-346.

Myers, Dowell. 1988. Building knowledge about quality of life for urban planning. Journal of the American Planning Association 54:347-358.

NRC (National Research Council). 1988. Air Pollution, the Automobile and Public Health. Washington, D.C.: National Academy Press. 704 pp.

NRC. 1997. Towards a Sustainable Future: Addressing the Long-Term Effects of Motor Vehicle Transportation on Climate and Ecology. Washington, D.C.: National Academy Press. 261 pp.

NRC 1999. Our Common Journey: A Transition Toward Sustainability. Washington, D.C.: National Academy Press. 363 pp.

Olson, Mancur. 1969. The relationships between economics and the other social sciences: The province of a social report. In Seymour Martin Lipset, ed., Politics and the Social Sciences. New York: Oxford University Press.

OMB (Office of Management and Budget). 1973. Social Indicators, 1973: Selected Statistics on Social Conditions and Trends in the United States. Washington, D.C.: U.S. Government Printing Office.

Pierce, Neal R., Curtis W. Johnson, and John Stuart Hall. 1993. Citistates: How Urban America Can Prosper in a Competitive World. Washington, D.C.: Seven Locks Press. 360 pp.

Scott, Allen J. 1998. Regions and the World Economy: The Coming Shape of Global Production, Competition, and Political Order. New York: Oxford University Press. 177 pp.

Smith, D. M. 1973. The Geography of Social Well-Being in the United States. New York: McGraw-Hill.

U.S. Department of Health, Education, and Welfare. 1969. Toward a Social Report. Washington, D.C.: U.S. Government Printing Office. 101 pp.

U.S. White House Task Force on Livable Communities. 2000. Building Livable Communities: Sustaining Prosperity, Improving Quality of Life, Building a Sense of Community. Washington, D.C.: Livable Communities Initiative.

Wackernagel, M., and W. Rees. 1996. Our Ecological Footprint: Reducing Human Impact on the Earth. Gabriola Island, B.C.: New Society Publishers. 160 pp.

World Commission on Environment and Development. 1987. Our Common Future. Oxford, U.K.: Oxford University Press. 383 pp.

Forest Hills Garden, sketch: Station Square, Forest Hills, Long Island (Borough of Queens), N.Y., 1910. Courtesy of the Frances Loeb Library Graduate School of Design, Harvard University.

2

The Importance of Place and Connectedness

PEOPLE AND PLACE

Place as Territory and Place as People

An understanding of place is fundamental to the concept of livability, including transportation-related aspects of livability. People live in places, move within and between places, and depend on the movement of goods to and from places. The individual characteristics of places are vital in determining quality of life. The internal structure of places and the differences between places also matter greatly in terms of socioeconomic inequality. However, it is difficult to measure what matters about places because their nature depends on both physical and social characteristics. They not only have a location, territorial domain, and natural environment, but also are social constructs, shaped by human behavior and interactions. One must avoid the temptation to think of place only as a location or a piece of territory, despite the fact that many data are collected and presented for a specific territory, especially territory delimited by political boundaries. A place is distinguished by its people, markets, governments, and institutions, as much as it is by its physical landscape and natural resources, transportation systems (including streets and roads), buildings, and boundaries. Like livability and sustainability, place is an ensemble concept.

A definition of place that recognizes the importance of location or territory and people has implications for the interpretation of livability and for the kind of data needed for place-based decision making. We may observe—in data or analysis—a fixed territory over time, but we are seldom observing a fixed collection of people. Even if we agree on how to measure livability for people who lived in Northam in 1990, and then for people who lived there in 2001, the collection of people is different at the two times, and the changes we describe are not necessarily relevant for every person there in 1990 or in 2001. A change in an indicator might not even be relevant for *most* of the people who lived there at either time, if the composition of the population changed rapidly. Interpretation is complicated even more if we rely on statistical averages to measure livability, as we do frequently in practice.

The character of a place, its identity, and its people's sense of rootedness are shaped by interactions within the place and with other places. This duality affects livability. In addition, places evolve over time, so connections across time are also important. The connection between Northam in 2001 and Northam in 1990 may be as important as the one between Northam in 2001 and Southam in 2001. One of the most important aspects of time is the considerable inertia (or path dependence) in urban settings, economic specialization, socioeconomic composition, institutions, and other characteristics of places.

These relationships can be described and analyzed in many different ways. No single way is completely satisfactory; everyone must draw artificial boundaries in order to describe the relationships between and among places. As already mentioned, place involves both territory and people. Another complication is that every person inhabits not a single place but a variety of places, not only over his or her lifetime, as is obvious, but also at any given moment. This phenomenon is due to the fact that people interact with the environment and with other people at many different scales simultaneously—in the home, the neighborhood, the town or city, the county, the state, the nation, and beyond.

It is useful to think of "vertical" and "horizontal" characteristics of places, to use the language adopted by some geographers (NRC, 1997; Hanson, 1999). Vertical refers to interactions between people, and between people and environment, within the confines of a given spatial concentration of population, production, and consumption. The word vertical is perhaps not all that evocative, but it does connote the accumulation or piling up of effects in a defined piece of territory. On the other hand, horizontal refers to interactions between places in the flows of people, goods, capital, and information. Horizontal characteristics of a place reflect relations of trade, commuting, migration, and communication. The vertical and horizontal labels are occasionally used in this discussion, although scholars sometimes use the word "place" to mean vertical and "space" to mean horizontal as shorthand expressions of these two different types of interactions.

History is also important to the concept of place. As time passes, places change, and every place has a legacy of past events. Both vertical and historical characteristics are partly the result of history. It is for those reasons that place biographies are a recognized genre of historical writing. Therefore, we need to add "historical" to vertical and horizontal. Discrete historical events, as well as the historical evolution of cultural norms and values, economic organization, and technologies, help shape places. Transformations related to transportation include the building of railroads, which altered fundamentally the economic situations of towns dependent on canals; the emergence of long-haul trucking and industrial agriculture, which irrevocably altered many railroad-oriented towns built to serve family farmsteads; and the development of efficient long-haul air transportation, which fostered the growth of tourist destinations such as Florida, Las Vegas, and Hawaii. In some places, the rise of the single-family suburban ideal home helped to devalue older, more traditional, urban neighborhoods; while in others, urban homesteading has recreated urban neighborhoods. The events that unfold throughout history change a place by changing the composition of its population because they induce movements in and out, and they also change the situations of many individuals who remain there. The range of topics relevant to an understanding of place is enormous and so is the scholarly literature, and it is not appropriate to rehearse large parts of it here. This report concentrates on a few of the most pertinent ideas rather than trying to cover every possible angle of place.

Places as Groups of Nodes in Networks

One way to think of place, both as location or territory and as people, is to start with the idea of nodes in networks. All persons participate in economic and social networks, and move—temporally and spatially—in and out of nodes in the networks. A node is a spatial and temporal cluster of interactions and common experiences, and it occurs wherever people meet together to work, buy and sell, study, talk, receive health care, cheer for a champion that represents them, or enjoy or fear the natural environment, for example. Then a person's place—his or her "here" or a community that he or she "belongs to"—is a group of nodes in which a person frequently spends time that are near each other spatially. We think of these places both as territory, which encloses the group of nodes, and as people, who occupy the same nodes with great frequency.

The terms "frequently" and "near" are dependent on the context of the question. A person is involved in many different nodes and places, at

different scales; for example, he or she is involved in the home, neighborhood, town or city, metropolitan area, state, country, and world. There is
no fixed answer to how best to group the nodes into meaningful places.
All are relevant to the person's sense of identity and quality of life, and all
are territories for which we need data in order to answer important questions. These places exist at multiple scales ranging from the micro (the
home as a node and thus a place important to the vast majority of people)
to the macro (the nation-state, or perhaps even group of nations as in
Europe). Thus, one might care a great deal about one small place, with
several interactions every day in a few square miles, and also care about a
larger place, with only a few interactions each month in a territory of
thousands of square miles. To repeat, the meaning of frequently and near
vary with the question at hand.

There are limits to this principle of multiplicity; not every location a
person visits, or might possibly visit, is equally meaningful or is meaningful in the same way as are the territories and people near to home. As a
first approximation, meaning declines as frequency of interaction and
nearness decline, although there are many exceptions. Ultimately, some
locations and some people are "other," or "over there," rather than "here."
Relationships with the over-theres are often based on economic trade,
occasional travel, or certain common experiences, rather than involving
frequent direct interaction.

However, the connections with distant places do affect one's own
place. Some distant places that tend to be out of sight and mind of local
residents in fact supply important resources, goods, and services to one's
own place, provide markets for the nearer place's own goods, assimilate
local wastes, or share the effects of a common government's taxes and
services. Livability of a place, *here,* is never completely independent of the
livability of places, *there.* The spatial dependence between places of similar scale is a determinant of the character of places at a *higher scale*: the
dependence between homes in a city, for example, shapes the character of
the entire city; the dependence between cities in a nation shapes the
character of the entire nation. Markets, movements of people, goods, and
information, and governments that encompass more than one place create
connections between places. Regional geographers and regional econo-
mists recognize some of these effects when they model agglomeration.
The connections mean that decisions in a single place at one moment—
about lifestyles, economic competitiveness, transportation choices for both
people and goods, and environmental amenities—affect the livability of
multiple other places at different scales and over the course of the future.

Our concern with nodes is consistent with the concern about time
geography (discussed in Chapter 3). The idea of places as clusters of

nodes is similar to that of Doreen Massey, who stated, "Instead, then, of thinking of places as areas with boundaries around, they can be imagined as articulated moments in networks of social relations and understandings . . . a sense of place . . . includes a consciousness of its links with the wider world . . ." (Massey, 1993, p. 66).

Multiplicity of Places and Scales: An Example

The following passage provides two hypothetical examples of the multiplicity of places, at different scales, that are important to people. A couple living in an apartment house in Milwaukee regards their neighborhood—their city block and a few adjoining blocks—as their place, because the nodes of home, common space of the apartment house, and stretches of sidewalk are important in their lives. However, they also regard the school district as their place, because another important node in their social network is the high school that their children attend. The school district is important even though the high school is several miles away from home—well out of the neighborhood. The couple regards both the neighborhood and the school district as their places, even though the two are based on different notions of near.

The couple also regards the city of Milwaukee and some of its suburbs as their place, perhaps because both of them work in that region—though at different sites—and the economic prosperity of the entire metropolitan area is important to them. A good local transportation system in the metropolitan area as a whole, for both people and goods, will increase their access to a range of public and private services, products, and cultural and natural amenities. The metropolitan region is also meaningful because of its cultural heritage, loyalty to certain sports teams, and homes of extended family members. The entire State of Wisconsin is also an important place for this couple in the sense that they feel they belong to it and visit other locations in the state frequently. All these different scales of place are relevant to a consideration of livability for this couple and how accessibility and transportation factor into this equation.

However, for another couple living in the same apartment house, the situation is different. Although they regard the neighborhood and the Milwaukee metropolitan region as their places, they do not care about the intermediate-scale place of the school district nor the high school, and do not even know what district they live in. They pay little attention to other areas in Wisconsin, although they do care about a region far away in the Pacific Northwest, which they visit frequently for extended periods.

Importance of Home in Identifying Place

While it is important to recognize the multiplicity of places in the life of each person, the notion of place is very much bound up with the notion of home. For most people, the home is one of the most important nodes, and the nature of social interaction and of mobility is that many other relevant nodes are close to home. To the question, In what place do you live? the first unprompted reply will identify some territory and population near home. This tendency is reinforced if the person works regularly and the work site is near the home; in this case it is common for the individual to say that the two nodes are in the same place, and this rough-and-ready notion underlies the official definition (in government statistics, for example) of metropolitan areas and local labor markets. This tendency is also reinforced if some individuals in the home attend school nearby. Other nodes are important—places to shop, worship, volunteer, get medical care, be entertained, play, commune with nature, and visit friends or family members—but it is fair to say that home, work site, and school are the most important nodes for a very large number of people. On the other hand, we cannot ignore the fact that one or more of those three basic nodes are not significant at all for some groups, such as the elderly.

Individuals do not have complete freedom to choose all the nodes or places that are important to them and that influence livability over their lifetimes. The following description of the concept of time geography illustrates the constraints and the importance of both space and time in conditioning human movement within and between places.

Time Geography and Movement in Time and Space

Torsten Hägerstrand and other geographers at Lund University in Sweden developed the concept of time geography in the 1960s (Hägerstrand, 1970). The space-time path is a central concept. Figure 2.1 illustrates a simple space-time path, showing how movement involves changes in both space and time. From the time-geographic perspective, the individual's choices of nodes of social interaction are functions of the locations in space and time that an individual's path can occupy, and the range of possible space-time paths is an important dimension of livability. The path's shape reflects the role of urban form, technology, and the institutions and regulations that facilitate or inhibit movement. A steepening (flattening) of the path indicates that the person must trade more (less) time for space in movement. There are three kinds of constraints that limit the range (Golledge and Stimson, 1997).

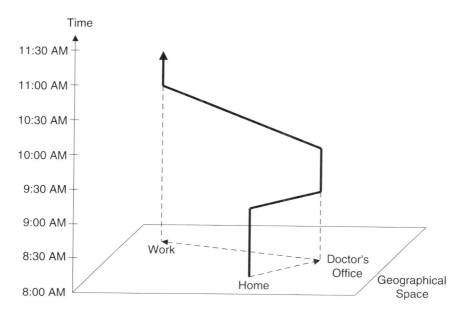

FIGURE 2.1 A space-time path.

Capability constraints limit an individual's participation in events in space and time by requiring that paths be in certain locations for fixed time intervals and by determining the steepness of the path when traveling outside those intervals. For example, capability constraints might lead one to devote a large amount time to physiological necessities such as sleeping, eating, and personal care, and these usually can occur at a limited number of locations, but transportation technologies could facilitate mobility from one of those locations.

Coupling constraints refer to the need to coordinate—to coincide in both space and time with other persons—in order to produce, consume, and participate in social activities. A job may require presence at a work site for a fixed number of hours per week. However, stores, medical facilities, and government offices are at limited numbers of locations in space and are open at limited hours.

Authority constraints are legal, economic, and social barriers that restrict the ability to be in particular locations at certain times. Gated suburban communities illustrate the attempt to impose authority constraints on nonresidents. The growth of spatial data in digital form and the development of sophisticated GIS have made it possible to model the time geographic aspects of people's lives that take account of these constraints, thus making it possible to analyze the livability of places in terms of the daily, weekly, and seasonal rhythms and patterns experienced by different individuals and by different demographic and social groups (Golledge and Stimson, 1997).

In Figure 2.1, time is short term, specifically diurnal. We can represent changes over time by putting several different paths on the same diagram, with each one applying to a different year, for example. One path is for one slice of time, say the current year, while others are for representative past or future years, and each shows a different diurnal pattern. The series of paths captures changes in the place and in the person, illustrating the evolution of the life course—for example, changes in the proportion of time spent working—and also changing natural and built environments, social structures, and transportation technology. For a person who changes places, the changes from one slice to another might be more marked because they also capture differences between places.

Political Places

Every brief definition has its problems, and an especially important complication for a definition of place based on nodes is created by political boundaries. In practice, including transportation planning, *political jurisdictions* are meaningful places for all residents, even if the residents do not frequently interact. These jurisdictions are towns and townships, cities, counties, school districts, special districts created for public utilities (including transportation utilities), and many others. Even the state and nation are important; for some persons, national-level policies are the ones that matter the most. The fact is that political units create many *common experiences* for people, such as common educational experiences (in school districts), common tax rates and regulations, and common standards of public goods and services provided in the jurisdiction. In creating these common experiences, governments affect the quality of life in many ways, for example, by affecting the quality of public services, by regulations, and by explicit and implicit redistribution of income.

Therefore, although one should resist the temptation to identify every place with some political jurisdiction, which is an unfortunate tendency in many sources of data, one must nevertheless recognize that political places are important. This clearly is necessary when considering any aspect of planning, financing, building, and operating transportation facilities including highways, public transportation, ports, and airports. Yet recognizing political jurisdictions and collecting data on them are not sufficient for answering questions about livability. A major feature of most political places is precisely defined boundaries that are fairly rigid over time. This characteristic distinguishes political places from other nodes of interaction whose boundaries are flexible or difficult to identify. The inflexibility of political boundaries, when coupled with constraints on residential mobility created by segmented housing markets and discrimination, has important implications for inequality because political units are so important in the distribution of resources. An exception is the boundaries of legislative districts, which change more frequently and play a role in how places are affected by national and state allocation and redistribution decisions.

Natural, Built, and Social Environments

The natural and built environments of a place are essential to social interactions. They are essential characteristics of the place, have powerful influences, and play a dual role.

1. These environments affect livability directly, by their inherent quality. For example, "air quality" and "water quality," in the sense of freedom from pollution, affect well-being directly by affecting health and the enjoyment of day-to-day living; the mere presence of aesthetically pleasing natural features and buildings has a positive effect on people's satisfaction and well-being.
2. These environments also affect the nature of the economic base, the productivity of market-oriented economic activity, and the efficiency of "household production" (where households pool their resources, combining the time of their members with items purchased in the market to produce fundamental goods such as recreation, education, and security).

Finally, the natural and built environments of a place show dynamic feedback effects, in that they condition individual behavior and are in turn affected and transformed by that behavior. They also impose inertia on social change and contribute to path dependence by virtue of containing some relatively long-lived features that human activity can change, but usually only gradually. Natural environments of places evolve over time because of ecosystem dynamics, extreme geophysical events (such as earthquakes), and anthropogenic or human-induced changes (pavement, river channeling, erosion, and other effects on soil fertility; removal of vegetation; and even climate change). However, in recent decades there has been an appropriately heightened sensitivity, especially to anthropogenic changes. In most places though, the human changes are slow; the natural setting provides long-lasting common elements in the history of the place; and these elements inevitably shape current attitudes and preferences, the ways in which people identify themselves, and the potential for economic successes. Although many important aspects of the natural environment are very slow to change, some natural features can change quickly. Air and water quality can deteriorate or improve relatively rapidly because pollution loads can change quickly and their accumulated stocks can have relatively quick effects.

While there is a sharp difference in degree, the built environment—buildings and infrastructure—is also relatively durable. The costs of change are lower than the costs of changes in the natural environment, but they are not trivial. These costs often inhibit change by making it economically impractical, even when possible in principle. Oftentimes, adding a new component requires substantial capital and produces returns only over a substantial period, thus inhibiting additions. If demolition of existing buildings or infrastructure is also required, there is even greater inhibition because the old capital has some productivity.

It is not only the durability of individual buildings, highways, streets, and other pieces of infrastructure that is relevant, but also the durability of entire assemblages. The durability of the built environment is a significant barrier to changes in the urban form of metropolitan areas that would make mass transportation economically viable. It is hard to change existing low-density, highway-oriented urban areas into more compact, high-density urban forms that would benefit from such transportation systems. Anthony Downs (1992, 1994, 2001) has discussed the various possibilities.

Structure, Institutions, and Agency

Economic, social, and political structures, on many scales influence economic production and consumption, flows of goods, and movement of populations between places. Public, private, and nonprofit institutions that mediate between social structures and individuals wield power in shaping allocation, distribution, investment, trade, and resource extraction decisions—decisions that can dramatically transform places. Large-scale structures can influence even the smallest places, something most places have become aware of when faced with economic changes lumped together under the rubric of "globalization." In turn, specific place-based agents—in business, government, and civic associations—influence institutional performance, policy, and direction and ultimately can affect even larger-scale structures. Thus, we have again a mutual feedback process in connection with the natural and the built environments.

Traditions, conventions, and norms also affect places, as emphasized in the recent literature on "social capital" (Coleman, 1988; Putnam, 1993, 2000; Becker, 1996). It is generally recognized that local social capital often

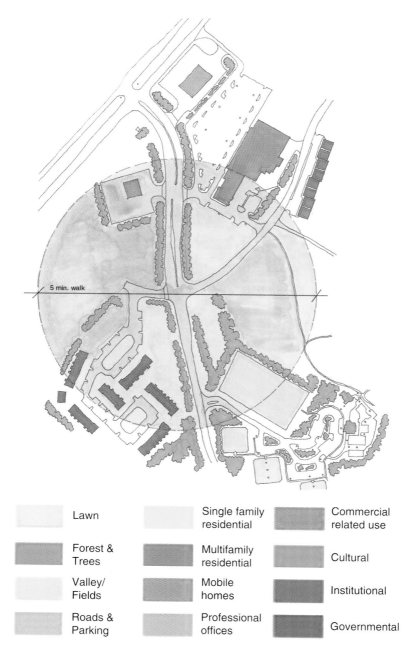

	Lawn		Single family residential		Commercial related use
	Forest & Trees		Multifamily residential		Cultural
	Valley/ Fields		Mobile homes		Institutional
	Roads & Parking		Professional offices		Governmental

PLATE 1 Thomas Jefferson Planning District EPI community element diagram—urban mixed use. SOURCE: Chris Sinclair, Renaissance Planning Group, Charlottesville, Virginia.

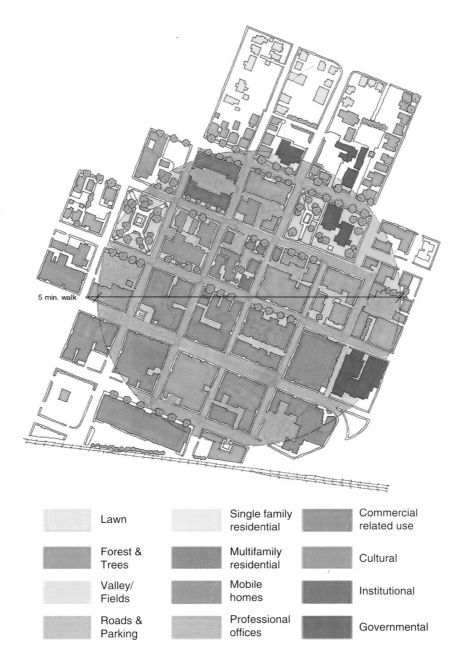

5 min. walk

	Lawn		Single family residential		Commercial related use
	Forest & Trees		Multifamily residential		Cultural
	Valley/ Fields		Mobile homes		Institutional
	Roads & Parking		Professional offices		Governmental

PLATE 2 Thomas Jefferson Planning District EPI community element diagram—suburban mixed use. SOURCE: Chris Sinclair, Renaissance Planning Group, Charlottesville, Virginia.

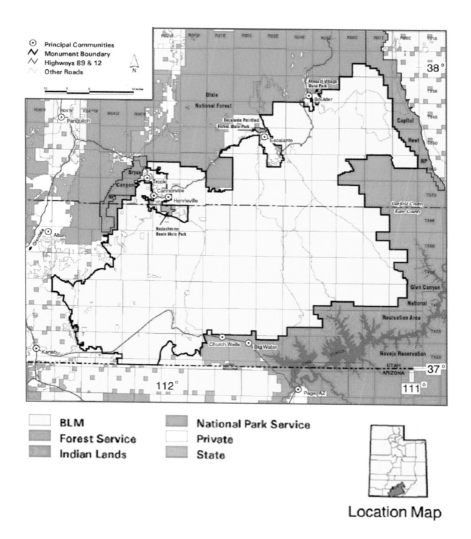

PLATE 3 Grand Staircase-Escalante Land Status GIS Map. Data were gathered from a variety of sources and integrated to provide a planning context. Data shown outside the monument may not have been verified. The map represents available information and should not be interpreted to alter existing authorities or management responsibilities. SOURCE: Produced by Grand Staircase-Escalante National Monument (1999).

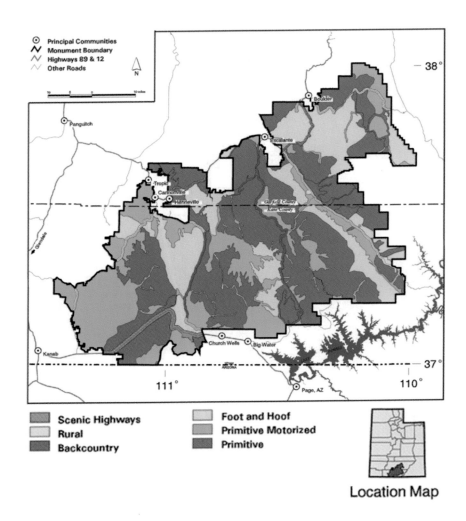

Legend (top left):
- ⊙ Principal Communities
- N Monument Boundary
- N Highways 89 & 12
- N Other Roads

Map labels:
Boulder, Panguitch, Escalante, Tropic, Cannonville, Henrieville, Garfield County, Kane County, Kanab, Church Wells, Big Water, Page, AZ, UTAH / ARIZONA

Coordinates: 38°, 37°, 111°, 110°

Legend (bottom):
- Scenic Highways
- Rural
- Backcountry
- Foot and Hoof
- Primitive Motorized
- Primitive

Location Map

PLATE 4 Grand Staircase-Escalante, Alternative E. Data were gathered from a variety of sources and integrated to provide a planning context. Data shown outside the monument may not have been verified. The map represents available information and should not be interpreted to alter existing authorities or management responsibilities. SOURCE: Produced by Grand Staircase-Escalante National Monument (1999).

helps to produce a distinctive community culture. This distinctive culture, which affects the local economy and especially local politics, is something that long-time residents, newcomers, and external scholarly observers alike can see. Newcomers may find themselves frustrated by "how things work" (or don't, in their view) and perhaps by not being able to fathom how things work within limited scopes of time. Tensions between longer-term residents and newcomers can make it difficult to achieve political compromise within a community, and tensions between communities with different cultures can make regional cooperation difficult. These tensions often arise in transportation decision making (e.g., choosing the route of a regional highway) just as they do when the issues concern local schools and other public services.

In this regard too, places at one scale affect places at another—the social capital in a large region, for example, depends in part on the social capital existing in smaller places within the same region. This social capital may have the same durability and slow-changing nature as the natural and built environments, but it is likely to have more in common with the built environment than the natural environment in this respect.

Rural Places

Rural places are especially difficult to define without using the flexible criteria of near and frequently in identifying the nodes that collectively make up a person's place. In rural areas, most people have relatively infrequent interaction with other people and the interaction takes place at widely scattered points in space. This is due in large part to the low density of population and the low spatial concentration of work sites. In some important agricultural regions, for example, farmers spend much of their work time in their own homes and make infrequent visits to other nodes. When they do visit other nodes, they must travel long distances— to sell their products, buy consumer goods and services, deal with government, or participate in nonprofit institutions. Their children often have long trips to and from school.

However, the sense of common purpose, identity, and rootedness may be just as strong in farming communities as in small towns or urban neighborhoods. Indeed, it has been suggested that some farming regions have a strong sense of place because their people see themselves as bound together by the common experience of dealing with the vagaries of nature. "Attachment to place can also emerge, paradoxically, from the experience of nature's intransigence" (Tuan, 1974, p. 97). Definitions of places and design of policies that affect places must give special recognition to rural areas, but as always, the criteria related to the terms near and frequent must be applied reasonably. For most purposes it is not useful to consider all of rural Nebraska as a single place, for example. The concept of community as place is discussed in more detail below.

Place and Community

In common parlance, community is often a synonym for place. Someone may say Southam is a pleasant place; another may say Southam is a pleasant community, and both mean exactly the same thing. Yet the people in a place, as defined here, may or may not share certain elements of community in another sense—that is, the sense of having common goals and values. This type of community feeling is not necessary for a territory and its people to qualify as a place for the purposes of this report. There are many communities that are not limited to any small piece of territory. There is, after all, the important case of "community without propinquity," as Melvin Webber put it (1973).

On the other hand, in many places a strong sense of community *does* develop. Often it arises from people's convictions about what the place is *not* and where it is not, as well as what it *is* (Allen et al., 1998, p. 82). This is an example of a more general principle that aspects of the unique and specific character of a place do not depend solely on the internal history of that place but also on the relations between that place and other places. The character of a place results from "a distinct *mixture* [italics in original] of wider and more local social relations," so that an understanding of sense of place "can only be constructed by linking that place to places beyond" (Massey, 1993, p. 68). Involvement in wider social relations—as in trade and investment, tourism and migration—does not necessarily impose homogeneity on places; rather it may actually help to reinforce uniqueness.

Sack (1997) suggests the metaphor of thick and thin places. Thin places are very specialized, have porous boundaries with the outside world because their people have extensive connections outside, and do not intrude much on people's consciousness. Thick places have people who are more inward looking and are more aware of their place in everyday life. "Thinner places can be . . . liberating, and its opposite—living in a closed and thick place with a rich web of stipulated meaning and routines—can be stultifying. . . . But [the freedom of thinner places] can also be unsettling, alienating, and lonely" (Sack, 1997, p. 10). To use Sack's terms, one might say that Webber's community without propinquity arises when people move about and communicate in large-scale places that have thickness for them, even though the place near home and most of the other smaller-scale places they are involved in are thin.

A strong sense of community, often considered an essential part of a sense of place, is a form of social capital and sometimes an important positive element in livability (Bolton, 1992). Unfortunately, this social capital often has negative effects on livability for some people (e.g., minorities or newcomers). Thinking of different geographical scales, it is possible that "even a large region can have a genuine sense of place as an agglomeration of senses of place in smaller localities and sub-regions [and] this agglomeration effect can operate even if it is only in the localities where intense and frequent social interactions take place. . . . Thus, one of the oldest distinctive notions in urban and regional economics, agglomeration, is relevant" (Bolton, 1992, p. 194). Here again is an example in which the spatial dependence between places of similar scale is a major determinant of the character of place at a higher scale.

TIME AND PLACE

One important aspect of time was raised in the discussion of the effect of durability of natural, built, and social environments. This section includes comments on other effects of time.

Changing Populations over Time: Movements In and Out

The passage of time not only affects the built and natural environmental settings of a place but also affects the local population. As the composition of the population changes, so do individuals' essential characteristics, including preferences for various public and private goods and for environmental and cultural amenities. Planners must cope with moving targets, speaking both metaphorically and literally. The legacy of the past may be long lasting for some portions of the population (long-time residents, in particular), but nearly irrelevant for others (recent in-migrants, for example), thus creating divisions and tensions. Changing populations further intensify the competition and conflict that characterize all places.

Some of the most dramatic examples of residential metamorphosis in recent decades have involved gentrification of poor urban neighborhoods. When gentrification is examined from the perspective of a particular piece of territory, the process may appear uniformly benign and beneficial. For example, social indicators begin to improve as neighborhoods gentrify. Aging and dilapidated housing stock is renovated or replaced; new purchasing power leads to commercial growth; and land values and rental costs increase. However, from the perspective of the people rather than territory, the displacement of lower-income individuals and their replacement by an influx of higher-income individuals contribute to the increases in rents and housing prices. These increases can cause considerable disruption of the social networks that the original residents developed over many years. The displaced individuals may not find adequate housing with a similar support structure.

When assessing the impact on livability of a discrete event that can be anticipated to have great and long-lasting effects, which people should "count" as the population of concern? Lakshmanan and Bolton (1986, p. 595) raise these questions: Should the focus be only on the people who are residents now? Should decisions be made based on the ones that are expected to live in the place at some future date in time? Or are the only persons who count those who not only live in the place now, but will continue to live there in the future? Clearly, planners do not focus only on current residents—they take the long view and consider likely in-migrants. Much planning is done precisely to attract new residents. Planners consider tourists and short-term visitors as well, especially if their spending adds to employment and tax revenue. Planners may also slight or underweight current residents who are likely to leave in the relatively near future.

Some common statistical indicators actually count the relevant population in a way not yet mentioned. Consider numbers such as total income, per capita income, poverty rate, illness due to poor environmental quality, and quality of public services per capita. These data are often available for each year and reflect the situation of all persons who live in the place *in that year*, no matter how long before or after they live there. The indicators do not allow one to discriminate among groups according to how long they lived in the place or whether their movements in and out were easy or were under duress. The problem arises both in interpreting historical data and in projecting livability over the future. It is important to have data that track individuals or at least certain groups of individuals.

It is often suggested that there is an opposition between people and place, as a way to highlight the problem of a changing population in a given political jurisdiction. It would be better to express the opposition as one between people and territory. The phrase "people prosperity versus place prosperity" actually refers to a conflict between two different kinds of policies. Both types of policies aim at helping people who are currently living in some place and who are in economic distress (Winnick, 1966; Bolton, 1992). People prosperity policies assist people whether or not they remain in a specific place. An example is general retraining that has a value even if the recipient decides to move elsewhere. Place prosperity policies are also aimed at people, but they confer benefits only if the recipient remains in a specific place; examples are subsidies for local job creation or public infrastructure.

Changing Populations over Time: Changing Minds

In addition to the effects of in-migration and out-migration, each individual also changes over his or her lifetime, and this too contributes to making the planners' clientele a moving target. Any description, any analysis, and any prescription for a place must take account of these changes. Some are natural changes over the individual's life course (Katz and Monk, 1993) and are somewhat predictable. These changes of course may be functions of gender, age at the start of the period, education and occupation, or other personal characteristics. The life course is dependent in large part on the career path, a concept well known in human capital theory and other areas of labor economics. Other changes are due to more abrupt alterations in economic situation or to shifts in social attitudes in the nation or region as a whole, and these are not very predictable.

The changes due to migration and turnabouts in preferences are related to each other in a significant way. Some change can prompt current residents to leave a place. Albert Hirschman (1970) distinguished "exit" and "voice." In a place facing difficult adjustment to long-term decline or to a short-term shock, many people must choose between exit and voice—leaving or remaining and participating in political processes that address the problem. The option to choose one course of action over another is significant, though this is never reflected in the readily available data. Many things affect choice, including the expected efficacy of voice if the person stays. If policy makers wish to retain populations, they have to design political processes that facilitate participation in the decision process.

Legibility: The Interaction Between Time and Place

One example of how the passage of time affects a place's character is the evolution of what Kevin Lynch (1960) called the "legibility" of a place. Legibility refers to "the ease with which [the city's] parts can be recognized and can be organized into a coherent pattern" (Lynch, 1960, pp. 2-3). Lynch saw this legibility as something that developed over time for city residents as a function of people's cognitive responses to the number and complexity of distinctive elements they encounter, including paths, edges, nodes, districts, and landmarks. The names of the elements are self-explanatory, with the exception of "districts," which refer to large areas in a city that "are recognized as having common, identifying character" (Lynch, 1960, p. 47). A district may get its common character from natural features, distinctive buildings, economic function, pervasive affluence, or pervasive poverty. High-poverty districts are major features of the modern city, and they are dramatic reminders of long-term historical processes shaped by discrimination, inequality of opportunity, durability of the built environment, presence or absence of social capital, and path dependence. Their residents often do not have adequate accessibility to jobs and essential amenities.

To Lynch's original list can be added the term "patch"—a small element of one type surrounded by other types. Examples include clusters of architectural styles, strip malls, highway medians, cemeteries, parks, wetlands, and wooded areas. Although patches can be created or lost quickly, paths connecting diverse patches can enhance the livability of a large, dense urban district.

Legibility can either add to or detract from the favorable qualities of a place, and historical processes are important in creating and preserving legibility. For example, some districts exhibit strong path interdependence, but others change fairly quickly due to population shifts.

In a recent European study, Geneviève Dubois-Taine (2001) described a system of "lived-in territories" or areas in space that are different and dispersed but connected by travel corridors. Examples include home and workplace, as well as town centers, urban villages, shopping centers, parks, areas of leisure, and places devoted to sharing experiences with others (concert halls, stadiums, etc.). These areas are like islands; they have distinctive character, yet mobility makes them contiguous to a degree, and the places and connections between them act as an integrated system (Dubois-Taine, 2001, p. 2). Travel between the territories may be by foot, bicycle, private car, or public transportation, but regardless of travel mode, the spaces between the lived-in territories are important features that help define the entire assemblage. Some writers in France (e.g., Viard, 1994) use the term "archipelago" to describe this system, although that word may underestimate the importance of connectedness between the lived-in territories.

This system of lived-in territories and connections has evolved to reflect several prominent characteristics of modern life: the increasing amount of non-work time, the decreasing density of urban settlements and increasing importance of built-up areas on the outskirts of older town centers, the desire to spend much of one's life near open space and other natural areas, and the general desire for independence and personal autonomy. People now want to live in an "all-options-open" place (Dubois-Taine, 2001, p. 2). The poor quality of local transportation accentuates inequalities in the availability of important options. There is also what Dubois-Taine calls the "desynchronization" of daily schedules: people are on the move much more and at many more times during the typical day or week, so that certain specific journeys make up a smaller proportion of total journeys and total time in movement (Dubois-Taine, 2001, p. 3). This is true, for example, of the home-to-work journey, traditionally the major focus of people's travel behavior and also of analysis and modeling. Thus, the space-time paths of people coincide less often than in the past. The many different lived-in territories and the different times people live in them, along with the nature of these modern travel corridors, underscore the need to focus on entire systems of lived-in territories.

PLACE AND SPACE: CONNECTIONS BETWEEN PLACES

Horizontal relationships between places are shaped by the flows of people, goods, and information and also by common experiences of different places located in a common political jurisdiction. Comparisons between places, linkages between them, and flows between them are ubiquitous. Much of the extensive scholarly literature is concerned with modeling economic specializations and the trade between places, which are relevant for work in cultural geography and sociology that explores the socioeconomic structure, character, and evolution of places over time. The literature also contains many models of systems of places, usually hierarchical in structure. In a familiar model of a place hierarchy, for example, each place is the market area of a particular set of firms; it distinguishes different classes or "orders" of such places, with the collected firms in each order producing all the goods that the firms in the next lower order do, plus other goods that no firm in the next lower order produces.

People, in their capacity as economic actors—whether managers of firms, workers, or retired persons choosing a place to live—are always making explicit comparisons of places. In a society that allows and even encourages mobility, it is essential that people evaluating their options have access to data on livability, in its many dimensions, in many different places. The choice between exit and voice, which affects how a place changes over time, never depends solely on internal or vertical characteristics—it is always made by comparing the place with other places, places one could move to, places one might move to. *Livability here* matters, but only in comparison with *livability there*.

Kinds of Linkages Between Places

Linkages related to transportation include personal travel, complementary and competitive connections in economic trade, movement of capital, and common experiences in political places. One common thread is the importance of air transportation, which looms larger in importance than in the previous discussion. However, transportation is not always a crucial factor in important linkages.

Personal Travel

People travel between places for many reasons, for example, to visit family, receive education, or participate in tourism or other recreational activities. Accordingly, ease and cost of travel is a factor in the livability a person enjoys. Over time, as extended families have continued to disperse, long-distance personal travel has become increasingly important. Therefore, air travel options and interstate highway systems have important implications for livability. Air travel has enabled growth of certain popular U.S. destinations, such as Florida, Las Vegas, and Hawaii, as well as many locations abroad. All of these places are important to tourists not only within the United States but also around the globe.

Economic Trade and Complementary Connections

Complementary refers to trade between producers of inputs and producers of final products. In any place, some business firms are producing final products and need transportation of inputs, whereas others are producing goods that will be inputs into final products made elsewhere. These inputs might include raw materials, energy sources, intermediate goods, and capital goods. The quality of freight transportation affects economic competitiveness, and in most places, rail, trucking, and air modes are relevant; water transportation also is important in some places. However, transportation of people is not a trivial concern, since managers, salespeople, and technicians often demand efficient travel to customers or suppliers, and here too the quality of air transportation is a factor.

Economic Trade and Competitive Connections

Most firms must compete for customers, and the quality of transportation affects competitiveness. This group of linkages is not sharply distinguishable from the previous ones, since producers of raw materials and intermediate goods must compete for customers, as do producers of final products. A variety of modes of freight transportation is especially important; additionally, air transportation of people is often an important factor.

Movement of Capital

It is useful to use the economist's distinction between capital, as generalized purchasing power, and capital goods, as tangible products such as machines and buildings that are produced by the economic system. The quality of communication matters for linkages in capital flows, but these capital flows are generally not as sensitive as other flows to the quality of transportation. The exceptions can be significant, however, especially in some places. For example, in the case of venture capital, the suppliers tend to be much more concentrated spatially than the recipients, yet both suppliers and recipients demand occasional face-to-face contact, requiring someone to travel.

Common Experience in Political Places

Connections between places are often created by political boundaries and a common government, even when there is no direct interaction or movement. The quality of public services, the protection of the environment, effects of regulation, and the combined effect of taxes and expenditures are determined by political places that encompass many smaller places. The inhabitants of these smaller places have limited power to affect the results. Residents of Northam and Southam have limited control over transportation decisions made in their state capital, but the residents of the two towns are inextricably linked together by the decisions made in Capital City. Travel within and between towns, travel in and out of the state, economic trade, and competition—all of these are affected by political jurisdictions.

Regional Identity

The distinguishing characteristics, including the identity, of larger places such as metropolitan areas or state and multistate regions depend on the relations and linkages between the smaller places in them. The perceived character of a large region, such as New England or the Great Plains, results from the simultaneous existence and interdependence of its large cities, small cities and towns, and rural areas and from interdependence between financial centers, manufacturing cities, and farming areas. A large region can have a clear identity and sense of place as an agglomeration of the identities of its smaller places.

Many elements of legibility in a larger region are assemblages of its smaller places. The major paths in the region are channels connecting the smaller places, for example, highways and river valleys. River valleys and basins in particular have long been identifying features of large regions. Bioregions are increasingly considered meaningful places as more people recognize the importance of river basins. The Connecticut River valley is an example of an identifying feature that helps the larger New England area. Such a valley may present a dilemma for the transportation planner: a natural corridor that cries out for efficient pavement, yet an element of legibility that should be altered with care. Edges are also good examples, as in coastal regions, and New England provides a convenient example in the Maine coast. The districts of a large-scale region are often clusters of towns, small cities, and rural areas, and the major landmarks are often single towns. Sometimes a landmark town is so small that it is only a patch when one considers the larger scale. An entire town may be one of the "lived-in territories" of the region. Sometimes a smaller place is important as a reminder of the region's history. Yi-Fu Tuan referred to "place as time made visible, or place as memorial to times past" (Tuan, 1977, p. 179).

Thus, again the variety of scales is important for legibility. In a small place, the elements of legibility may be a river walkway, a town square, a college campus, a mountain, or a park. In a large region, they may be a river valley, an ocean coast, a college town, a mountain range, an emerald necklace of parks in several towns, or a subregion featuring many farms and small towns.

The connections between these smaller places within the larger one change over time. Smaller places may change greatly, sometimes with marked effect on the character of the larger region. One town's economic specialization may change from manufacturing to retail trade or residential, with little impact on the region. Yet a rural district may change from primarily agricultural to primarily tourist, and the loss of rurality and the increases in congestion have a significant deleterious effect. The same can happen if a rural district with farms or a small town is transformed into an edge city by suburban expansion from a large, distant city by construction of a superhighway and interchange. Transportation routes and facilities can have a major effect on the character of the entire region.

REFERENCES

Allen, J., D. Massey, and A. Cochrane. 1998. Rethinking the Region. New York: Routledge.

Becker, G. 1996. Preferences and values. Chapter 1 in Accounting for Tastes. Cambridge, Mass.: Harvard University Press. 268 pp.

Bolton, R. 1992. "Place prosperity" vs. "people prosperity" revisited: An old issue with a new angle. Urban Studies 29:185-203.

Coleman, J. S. 1988. Social capital in the creation of human capital. American Journal of Sociology 94:S95-S120.

Downs, A. 1992. Stuck in Traffic: Coping with Peak-Hour Traffic Congestion. Washington, D.C.: Brookings Institution, and Cambridge, Mass.: Lincoln Institute of Land Policy. 210 pp.

Downs, A. 1994. New Visions for Metropolitan America. Washington, D.C.: Brookings Institution, and Cambridge, Mass.: Lincoln Institute of Land Policy. 256 pp.

Downs, A. 2001. The Future of U.S. Ground Transportation from 2000 to 2020. Remarks to the U.S. House of Representatives Committee on Transportation and Infrastructure, Subcommittee on Highways and Transit, March 22. Available at http://www.brookings.edu/views/testimony/downs/20010322.htm. Accessed September 26, 2001.

Dubois-Taine, G. 2001. An analysis of the human settlements in France: Ville emergente. Western Regional Science Association Meeting, Palm Springs, Calif., February.

Golledge, R., and R. Stimson. 1997. Spatial Behavior: A Geographic Perspective, 2nd edition. New York: Guilford. 620 pp.

Hägerstrand, T. 1970. What about people in regional science? Papers of the Regional Science Association 24:7-21.

Hanson, S. 1999. Isms and schisms: Healing the rift between the nature-society and space-society traditions in human geography. Annals of the Association of American Geographers 89:133-143.

Hirschman, A. 1970. Exit, Voice, and Loyalty: Responses to Decline in Firms, Organizations, and States. Cambridge, Mass.: Harvard University Press. 162 pp.

Katz, C., and J. Monk, eds. 1993. Full Circles: Geographies of Women over the Life Course. New York: Routledge. 317 pp.

Lakshmanan, T., and R. Bolton. 1986. Regional energy and environmental analysis. Pp. 581-628 in P. Nijkamp, ed., Handbook of Regional and Urban Economics, Vol. 1: Regional Economics. Amsterdam: North Holland Press.

Lynch, K. 1960. The Image of the City. Cambridge, Mass.: MIT Press. 194 pp.

Massey, D. 1993. Power-geometry and a progressive sense of place. Pp. 59-69 in J. Bird, B. Curtis, T. Putnam, G. Robertson, and L. Tickner, eds., Mapping the Futures: Local Cultures, Global Change. New York: Routledge.

Putnam, R. 1993. Making Democracy Work: Civic Traditions in Modern Italy. Princeton, N.J.: Princeton University Press. 258 pp.

Putnam, R. 2000. Bowling Alone: The Collapse and Revival of American Community. New York: Simon and Schuster. 541 pp.

NRC (National Research Council). 1997. Rediscovering Geography: New Relevance for Science and Society. Washington, D.C.: National Academy Press. 234 pp.

Sack, R. 1997. Homo Geographicus. Baltimore, Md.: Johns Hopkins University Press. 292 pp.

Tuan, Y.-F. 1974. Topophilia: A Study of Environmental Perception, Attitudes, and Values. Englewood Cliffs, N.J.: Prentice-Hall.

Tuan, Y.-F. 1977. Space and Place: The Perspective of Experience. Minneapolis, Minn.: University of Minnesota Press.

Viard, J. 1994. La société d'archipel ou les territoires du village global. Éditions de L'Aube. Paris: La Tour d'Aigues.

Webber, M. W. 1973. Order in diversity: Community without propinquity. Pp. 23-54 in L. Wingo, Jr., ed., Cities and Space: The Future Use of Urban Land, Essays from the Fourth Annual Resources for the Future Forum. Baltimore, Md.: Johns Hopkins Press for Resources for the Future.

Winnick, L. 1966. Place prosperity vs. people prosperity: Welfare considerations in the geographic redistribution of economic activity. Pp. 273-283 in Real Estate Research Program, Essays in Urban Land Economics in Honor of the Sixty-Fifth Birthday of Leo Grebler. Los Angeles: University of California.

Expressways and Byways, 1971, by Edward Koren. Courtesy of *New Yorker* magazine.

3

Measurement and Analysis of Livability

The second chapter emphasized that livability is a spatial and temporal phenomenon. This chapter discusses some of the issues involved in measuring and analyzing livability, including how to measure place-based indicators. Place-based indicators (and indeed any place-based measurements) involve issues such as the effects of arbitrary geographic boundaries and units, the possibility of ecological fallacy, deciding when measurement should occur, reconciling incompatible data units, and considering spatial data in statistical methods.

Issues involved in measuring accessibility to opportunities and to resources are also discussed. Individual accessibility to opportunities and resources is a central component of livability. However, "accessibility" is a multifaceted concept involving some challenging measurement issues, for example, space-time accessibility measures. These measures derive from the time geographic perspective discussed in Chapter 2 and capture the effects of individual activity schedules on accessibility. Since daily and weekly activity schedules vary widely by socioeconomic variables such as class, life cycle, culture, and gender roles, space-time accessibility measures are sensitive to individual differences in accessibility. Space-time accessibility measures can support livability measures that take into account the varying access to resources and opportunities between social and demographic groups in a community. A case study in Box 3.1 describes the planning of a national monument area in southern Utah, which allowed diverse groups to access geospatial data that provided information needed to fully participate in the monument planning process.

BOX 3.1
Grand Staircase-Escalante National Monument

Grand Staircase-Escalante National Monument comprises 1.7 million acres of public land in southern Utah and was designated a national monument by President Clinton. This designation marked the beginning of a three-year process during which the Bureau of Land Management (BLM) worked with state and local governments and other interests to set up a land management process. To meet this goal, the planning team recognized that an important facet of the process involved making the pertinent spatial data accessible to the large community of data users and interest groups. Digital data presented electronically over the Internet were determined to best facilitate the provision of information in a quick, efficient, and effective manner. The process relied on assistance from the Federal Geographic Data Committee and on National Spatial Data Infrastructure (NSDI) principles and technologies.

The opportunity and need for sharing geospatial data led to a unique collaborative planning process. A 17-member planning team solicited public input, developed issues, and prepared management alternatives to create a draft plan. The planning team established a strategy that employed a Geographic Information System (GIS) workstation outside the BLM network and was connected to the State of Utah's Wide Area Network and the Internet. The draft plan was then posted on the Internet to receive comments during a 120-day public comment period. The benefits of data sharing during this process were identified and evaluated by local decision makers,

(A) No Mans Mesa. Photograph by Jerry Sintz.

continued

(B) Metate Arch. Photograph by Jerry Sintz.

continued

BOX 3.1 Continued

local residents, state and federal employees, recreationists, environmental groups, and the planning team through personal interviews.

Construction of a geospatial database for planning the monument consisted of assembling data from a variety of sources. Data were converted from the old Bureau of Land Management GIS Maps Overlay and Statistical System, and other data layers were acquired from federal and state agencies. A primary concern was that the geospatial data not be duplicated, especially base or framework data. A significant barrier to the ability to share the monument project's geospatial database was that the BLM network security policy prohibited access to geospatial data residing in the planning office for users outside the wide-area network. To overcome the security policy, a dedicated GIS workstation was installed in the Cedar City office but outside of the BLM network.

During the development of the draft management plan, approximately 30 GIS data layers were available to download on-line in ARC/INFO export format. Data utilized in this assessment included fish and wildlife, plants, geology, objects of historic and scientific interest, road locations, mining activity, grazing leases, wild and scenic rivers, wilderness study areas, and recreation areas. The planning team also prepared an archive project, which can be viewed on-line using the archive Internet map server. Much of the data were placed on the web where they could be downloaded and analyzed by stakeholders. The Wilderness Society and other environ-

(C) Grosvenor Arch. Photograph by Jerry Sintz

continued

BOX 3.1 Continued

mental groups were most proficient at taking advantage of this information. They thought that access to data for analysis much improved their ability to make effective comments on the draft plan.

The general public mostly responded to maps showing roads and plan alternatives. Citizens were able to use their own knowledge of the area to comment on the appropriateness of specific plans. In many cases, their comments filled in gaps in the knowledge of the planning group; not all useful data are available to governments trying to achieve a successful planning effort. In other cases, seeing plan details diffused fears that the general public had about the loss of access to favorite sites within the monument.

As a result of the public input, the planning team added and removed several roads from the preferred transportation alternative coverage based on map-driven comments from the public comment period. Administrative roads in the accepted alternative were reduced from 310 miles in the draft plan to 192 miles in the proposed plan. In addition, changes and buffer zones were added to the monument management zones and boundaries based on public comment. More than 6,800 comments were received regarding the draft plan.

A qualitative analysis of the process found the following benefits: increased participation in the planning process, increased understanding of the plan, more substantive comments, improved communication, improved geospatial database for the monument, and an improved proposed plan. The paper and electronic GIS maps increased citizens' understanding of the plan. Individuals were able to get a clear picture of the process that led up to policy decisions. In addition, GIS use increased among stakeholder groups as a result of this data sharing pilot project.

GIS maps improved the planning process by providing stakeholders with a common language—GIS allowed them to discuss issues, rather than dispute location of features. The public found visual information easier to understand than written chapters. Individuals found that the increased perspective on the implications of various alternatives clarified their initial ideas about the plan. See examples of these collaborative GIS efforts on Plates 3, 4, and 5

SOURCE: BLM (1999).

DEVELOPING PLACE-BASED INDICATORS

Most place-based analyses use data reported at an aggregate level for some kind of geographic area. Examples include census tracts, census block groups, traffic assignment zones, school districts, or political units such as municipalities and counties. It is not always the case that these "administrative" areas match well with the definition of places as described in the previous chapter. These areas also may not adequately represent characteristics or needs of individuals. A discussion of some of the problems associated with measuring and analyzing the attributes of places follows.

Arbitrary Geographic Boundaries

Geographic boundaries created for measurement or administrative purposes can create misleading spatial patterns in geographic phenomena. Trying to place an external boundary around a study region can create two artificial effects in measurement and analysis. One is an "edge effect" created by ignoring interdependences that occur outside the bounded region. A second effect is the artificial shape imposed by the boundary. Shape can affect the measurement of spatial point patterns (e.g., reported crime locations) since these compare the points' locations relative to area. For example, as spatial units become more elongated, point pattern statistics tend to report higher levels of clustering for the same point pattern within that unit (Fotheringham and Rogerson, 1993).

Shape relative to area can also affect the measurement of interactions (e.g., origin-destination flows) since these are often recorded only when they cross an artificial boundary. Information about shape and area can be exploited to more accurately estimate distances from travel surveys (Rogerson, 1990) or to locate traffic counters, travel survey stations, or traffic monitoring systems (Kirby, 1997).

The problem of defining "urbanized areas" provides a relevant example of geographic bounding problems. The U.S. Census defines urbanized areas as jurisdictions with 1,000 persons or more per square mile. Figure 3.1 illustrates U.S. Census urbanized area boundaries for a portion of the Rocky Mountain Front Range that includes Ft. Collins and Greely, Colorado. Purple lines indicate the urbanized area boundaries, red shading indicates urban land use, orange shading indicates suburban land use; and yellow shading indicates exurban land uses. As can be seen, the census definition of urbanized area is problematic. Similarly, urban livability indicators such as measures of sprawl often ignore interdependences and interactions with proximal (or nearby) rural areas (Theobald, 2001).

There are several strategies for resolving geographic boundary problems in measurement and analysis (see Griffith, 1983; Griffith and Amrhein, 1983; Martin, 1987; Wong and Fotheringham, 1990). A practical computational strategy is to use GIS tools to manipulate boundaries systematically and to conduct the measurement and analysis given these different boundaries. This provides a sensitivity analysis of the indicator with respect to boundary definitions. Without this type of sensitivity analysis, the reliability and robustness of place-based livability measures that rely on administrative boundaries are unclear.

FIGURE 3.1 Geographic underbounding and overbounding in Ft. Collins, Colorado. SOURCE: Theobald (2001).

Arbitrary Geographic Units

Closely related to artificial boundaries is the problem of the effect of arbitrary geographic units on place-based measurement and analysis. Data for livability indicators are often spatially aggregated according to a defined spatial zoning system such as census tracts, census block groups, school districts, or political units such as municipalities or counties. These units can be meaningful in reality; for example, municipalities correspond to geographies of taxation and service provision. Environmental regions, such as watersheds, can be identified easily and bounded, allowing some physical variables to be measured nonarbitrarily. However, the "coarseness," created by spatially aggregated reporting units is often a barrier to understanding the spatial variation of many important social variables. The problem arises when measuring both the average level of a variable and its unequal distribution over the population.

Problems associated with arbitrary geographic units are known as the *modifiable areal unit problem* (MAUP) in the spatial analysis and quantitative geography literatures. The MAUP occurs when analyzing data that are recorded (or reported) for arbitrary spatial units. If the spatial zoning system is arbitrary or "modifiable," then the results of any measurement or analysis based on those units are also arbitrary or modifiable (see Miller, 1999a).

The MAUP has two dimensions. One dimension is *scale*: this relates to the level of spatial aggregation in the data. For example, in a multicounty metropolitan area, we might have data for each city, town, and township, or we might have only an average for each county. The other dimension is *zoning*, which refers to changes in the spatial partitioning given a fixed level of spatial aggregation (Openshaw and Taylor, 1979; Wong and Amrhein, 1996). For example, we might have data that show the averages for groupings such as center city and inner and outer suburbs, or data showing averages for central city and eastern and western suburbs, where these groupings are all roughly equal in size.

The MAUP can be illustrated using an example based on Monmonier (1996, pp. 140-145). Figure 3.2 is a map of a region of 16 towns that vary in population size. Assume that Towns 4, 10, and 13 are considerably larger in population than the rest. Also assume that a livability index has

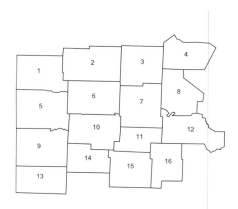

FIGURE 3.2 A region of 16 towns for the modifiable areal unit example.

been calculated for each town based on an average value per household. This index would be based on factors agreed upon by the communities involved as indicators of livability. For the purposes of this discussion, it does not matter which indicators or set of indicators was chosen by these towns for this comparison. Figure 3.3 maps the livability index for each town. There are three levels of the index: (i) *low*—index varies between 8 and 12; (ii) *medium*—index varies between 18 and 22; (iii) *high*—index varies between 28 and 33.

Note that the sharp differences between low, medium, and high categories means that a large change in a town's index is required to change its category. This example shows that the MAUP is independent of the imprecision in choosing the dividing lines between low, medium, and high. The spatial pattern of livability in Figure 3.3 shows a general north-south variation. This approach is not perfect, however; Towns 1 and 15 are notable departures.

Figure 3.4 shows the calculated livability categories when grouping towns into three north-south regions. The spatial pattern of livability now shows an *exact* north-south variation, hiding the fact that several towns are not typical of their regions. For example, livability seems to jump *two* levels in Town 1 and to drop *two* levels in Town 15. Figure 3.5 maps the index for a different grouping into three east-west regions. This grouping creates even more dramatic change in apparent livability: 11 of the 13 towns have different classifications relative to those in Figure 3.3. Town 16

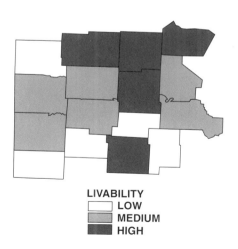

LIVABILITY
LOW
MEDIUM
HIGH

FIGURE 3.3 Hypothetical livability index mapped for the 16 towns.

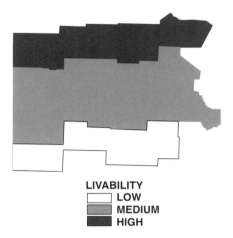

FIGURE 3.4 Hypothetical livability index mapped for a north-south aggregation.

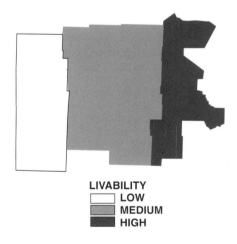

FIGURE 3.5 Hypothetical livability index mapped for an east-west aggregation.

jumps two levels higher compared than in Figure 3.3. However, Figure 3.5 represents the large towns (Towns 4, 10, and 13) accurately.

Figures 3.4 and 3.5 show both aggregation effects and zoning effects. Compared to Figure 3.3, both show the effect of aggregation. Compared to each other, they show the effect of zoning since both have the same degree of aggregation (two four-town groupings and one eight-town grouping) yet give different pictures of livability in many towns.

There are many other possibilities for zoning and aggregation, each of which can create different representations of livability. For example, if all 16 towns are made into a single group (perhaps to compare them to another region not shown here), the single group would have a medium level of livability based on the index. As another example, Figure 3.6 shows the results of grouping only three towns into a single metropolitan area of one large town (Town 10) plus two smaller ones (Towns 14 and 15). In this case, the medium rating of the special area overstates the livability index for Town 14 and understates it for Town 15 but is accurate for Town 10. While this hypothetical example and the maps illustrate the point for towns, livability can be affected strongly by smaller-scale changes. The livability of two neighboring houses on the same street could be assessed very differently, or whole areas of a city might be assessed as having a low livability index without any discussion of how to change these factors. Appropriate treatment of scale is also important for smaller areas such as neighborhoods and, indeed, for areal units of any size.

The simple examples in Figures 3.2 through 3.6 illustrate that place-based livability measurements are partially an artifact of the spatial reporting units. We can create substantially different patterns of livability

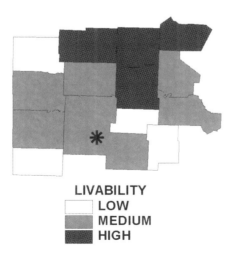

LIVABILITY
LOW
MEDIUM
HIGH

FIGURE 3.6 Hypothetical livability index mapped for a metropolitan-nonmetropolitan aggregation.

from the same data, simply by changing the spatial units. This strategy brings into serious question the reliability and robustness of any place-based livability measurement that uses spatially aggregated data.

What can be done about the modifiable areal unit problem when measuring and analyzing livability? One strategy is to attempt to develop optimal spatial units for the particular problem being addressed. This requires assembling smaller spatial units into larger spatial units in order to optimize some criterion (e.g., equal proportion of minority groups). Horn (1995), Openshaw (1977, 1978), and Openshaw and Rao (1995) discuss methods for optimal spatial unit design. The multidimensional nature of livability creates some problems, since optimal spatial unit design becomes more difficult, and some cases became impossible as the number of variables increases (although correlations among variables can reduce this complexity).

A second strategy is to assess the impacts of the arbitrary zoning system on the measured livability indicators. This is similar to the sensitivity analysis strategy discussed with respect to arbitrary geographic boundaries. GISs can support sensitivity analysis of MAUP effects in livability analysis through their ability to reorganize spatial data as well as visualize and communicate results (Fotheringham and Rogerson, 1993). Fotheringham and Wong (1991) provide a good illustration of sensitivity analysis with respect to spatial aggregation and zoning.

Ecological Fallacy

Another issue that is related to problems with aggregate geographic units is the *ecological fallacy*. The ecological fallacy occurs when the characteristics of individuals are inferred from aggregate data. For example, it can be tempting to conclude that a livability attribute calculated from aggregate data for a region, city, census tract, or census block reasonably describes the situation of most individuals within that geographic unit. In fact, of course, aggregate measures can mask a great deal of variability among individuals (Knox, 1978). This danger is common to all analyses with aggregate data, whether spatial or nonspatial.

It is difficult to argue that either a place-based or a person-based perspective is more appropriate. Each perspective provides a different lens through which to view livability. For example, using a person-based perspective alone may lead us to commit an *individualistic fallacy* by ignoring holistic factors that emerge at aggregate levels (Johnson, 1986). Both place-based and person-based perspectives are necessary for appropriate analysis of livability. For example, a pure individualistic perspective ignores the social networks and informal social capital that can develop in some neighborhoods.

Time of Measurement

The time geographic perspective discussed in the previous chapter tells us that human settlement landscapes are affected by the timing of events as much as by the spacing of people, activities, and structures.

We can analyze space-time human geographies from both people-based and place-based perspectives. In a people-based strategy, we analyze and visualize individual space-time paths, trying to understand individual movements and constraints on movements. The activity diary data collected for many years by local metropolitan planning organizations and departments of transportation can support livability analysis from that perspective. These data track individual movements and activities in time and space in order to plan transportation infrastructure and formulate transportation policy that are sensitive to the required and desired activities that comprise individuals' lives. The development and deployment of *position-aware technologies* such as in-vehicle navigation systems, cellular telephones, personal digital assistants, and wireless Internet clients are lowering the cost required to conduct detailed studies of the space-time human geographies of cities (Smyth, 2001).

GISs can be used to visualize and explore these space-time trajectory data. We can visualize time-space paths in a static mode using a three-dimensional model of space-time that shows the entire path within a geographic space and a fixed domain of time (Forer, 1998). Another possibility is animated maps that show the dynamic evolution of these paths in geographic space over time (van der Knaap, 1997; Kwan, 2000a). The increasing possibilities for collecting space-time path data in real time through intelligent transportation systems, location-based services, and other position-aware technologies mean that animation and other exploratory geographic visualization techniques will become essential for understanding space-time path data.

A place-based strategy is to aggregate the space-time paths into *space-time units* using temporal measurements taken at discrete time intervals for the spatial reporting units (Taylor and Parkes, 1975). Examples of space-time units are census block groups with attributes measured at different representative times such as "weekday morning," "weekday evening," "weekend morning," and "weekend evening." In contrast, the standard census practice of recording attributes based on home location assumes a particular time (e.g., weekday evening) that may not accurately represent the unit over the daily and weekly clocks. A central business district can appear relatively empty based on this measure. Also, neighborhoods with significant social, cultural, and entertainment activities, such as restaurants and nightclubs, may have completely different demographics on weekend evenings than during most other time of the week.

We can analyze the aggregate data using statistical techniques (while being mindful of arbitrary boundary and unit problems, as well as dependences in the data). The space-time units can show diurnal patterns in the social geography of the city as well as interactions between activities, social settings, and urban form. They allow measurement and prediction of the impact of changes in demographics, socioeconomic structures, and activity patterns within the urban environment as well as time-varying demands for transportation infrastructure. Longitudinal studies can allow assessment of the effect of long-term changes on livability; for example, the effects of changing demographics, continuing intensive use of the automobile, the growth of multi-income households and participation of women in the labor force, and the wider use of telecommunication technologies (Goodchild and Janelle, 1984; Janelle et al., 1998).

Incompatible Data Units

Livability and sustainability are complex phenomena measured across multiple dimensions. Geographical data are often collected using different, sometimes arbitrary, spatial units. For example, data available from a census, based on census tracts or other secondary sources, may not match the traffic analysis zones used by transportation planners in a transportation department or a metropolitan planning organization (MPO). Integrating these data means resolving different spatial recording systems. *Spatial basis transfer* is the term used to describe the conversion of data from one spatial system to another. If spatial basis transfer is not conducted properly, the resulting place-based measurements can be arbitrary, and even misleading, since the geographic framework for the measure is distorted.

Sometimes there is a need to transfer data from one area (the source zone) and apply them to another (the target zone). If the target zones nest perfectly within the source zones, this process is straightforward. If the nesting is not perfect, then *areal interpolation* is required (Goodchild and Lam, 1980). The appropriate method for interpolating data from source zones to target units depends on beliefs or assumptions about the spatial variation of the data within these zones (Goodchild et al., 1993). If both the source and the target zones are relatively homogeneous, the method of *areal weighting* can be used. This method distributes the data in the source zones to the target zones based on the share of the source zone within each target zone (see Goodchild and Lam, 1980). If the source zones are not homogeneous and there are other data that say something about the distribution of the variable within each zone (e.g., housing value as a surrogate for household income), statistical techniques such as the *expectation-maximization* algorithm can be used (see Flowerdew et al.,

1991). If neither the source zones nor target zones are homogeneous but we have access to a third set of zones with a surrogate variable that has a constant density, these *control zones* can be used in an intermediate stage of the areal weighting technique to interpolate in two steps, first to the control zones and then to the target zones (Goodchild et al., 1993).

Imagery derived from remote sensing platforms is an increasingly viable source of socioeconomic as well as physical data. Traditional satellite-based remote sensor systems were limited to spatial resolution no higher than 10 meters. New high-resolution sensing systems can achieve spatial resolutions 1 meter higher. Spectral resolution is also improving: new hyperspectral sensor systems such as the Airborne Visible InfraRed Imaging Spectrometer (AVIRIS) capture more than 200 very narrow bands, providing a detailed spectral signature that allows discrimination to the subpixel level (i.e., the groundcover "mix" within a pixel). Jensen and Cowen (1999) discuss minimum spatial, temporal, and spectral resolutions required in remote sensing systems to extract urban and suburban infrastructure. Mesev, et al. (1996) discuss methods for inferring urban socioeconomic data from remote sensing imagery.

Spatial-Temporal Data and Inferential Statistics

The connectedness of livability in space and time is concerned with two other issues related to inferential statistics: namely, *spatial dependence* and *spatial heterogeneity*. We often refer to spatial dependence as *spatial autocorrelation* when discussing this property from a statistical perspective. Spatial dependence refers to the tendency of individuals or geographical units that are proximal in space to exhibit similar characteristics. Closely related is *temporal dependence* or temporal autocorrelation.

Spatial heterogeneity relates to the inadequacy of overall (system-wide) parameters in describing a specific phenomenon at individual locations. Spatial heterogeneity can occur for two reasons (Fotheringham, 2000). One reason is that some relationships are intrinsically different across space; for example, people's behavior may vary by community or administrative, political, economic, and other boundaries or contexts. This creates contextually different responses to the same stimuli. Measuring spatial heterogeneity is a precursor to more intensive study to identify these contextual effects. Another reason is that the statistical model is not specified properly; one or more variables are missing or do not have the correct functional form. This statistical model can lead to misleading conclusions from the model. A classic example is a disaggregate spatial interaction ("gravity") model leading to the conclusion that people in Albany, New York, are "jet-setters" compared to those in Los Angeles, California (Fotheringham, 1981). In this case, we must capture the spatial heterogeneity in the model to account for the missing or incorrectly specified effects.

Multivariate statistical techniques such as regression analysis are often used to test causal relationships between livability indicators and fiscal, social, economic, and environmental variables. These methods can be used to determine how much of the variability is attributable to specific factors. Standard multivariate statistical methods make the assumption that all observations are independent of one another, that is, they do not vary one with another. With geographic data, independence cannot always be assumed because of spatial dependence, whereby factors do vary in relation to one another. Spatial dependence in the observations means that parameter estimates and significance tests are unreliable (Anselin and Griffith, 1998). It does not necessarily affect the model's predictive accuracy but does seriously undermine the ability to use calibrated parameters to explain the relative causal effects of the independent variables.

There are many different methods for dealing with the challenges of measuring spatial dependence and spatial heterogeneity (see Getis and Ord, 1992; Anselin, 1995; Ord and Getis, 1995). Problems associated with spatial dependence among observations in multivariate regression and related techniques can be resolved by including spatial autocorrelation in the dependent variable, independent variables, error terms, or some combination (Anselin, 1988, 1993). Spatial dependence and spatial heterogeneity can be captured simultaneously using *geographically weighted regression*. Geographically weighted regression generates disaggregate, location-based regression parameters that show spatial variations in the relationships between the independent variables and the dependent variable (see Brunsdon et al., 1996). Geographically weighted regression results are easily mapped, creating powerful geographic visualizations to highlight spatial trends and spatial variations, and to identify local exceptions to these relationships (Fotheringham, 2000).

MEASURING ACCESSIBILITY

Accessibility is a key component of livability that implicitly or explicitly underlies many measures and analyses of livability. Accessibility is also closely intertwined with policies that intentionally or unintentionally influence livability.

Many livability measures assume that the resources and opportunities at a place are perfectly available to individuals who are "proximal" to that location. New policies that attempt to influence livability also make this assumption. However, factors other than propinquity can affect the ability of individuals to obtain resources and opportunities. This result means that measures can overestimate livability and the effectiveness of related policies by masking individual variations in the benefits actually obtained from resources and opportunities.

Since accessibility is central to urban theory and policy, there is a long history of attempts to measure this concept. Accessibility can be based on *potential* or on *outcomes* (Scott, 2000). Potential measures attempt to quantify the ability of locations or individuals to interaction with other locations or individuals. Examples include time model-based ("isochrones") and spatial interaction ("gravity") model-based measures, such as the well-known Hansen potential measure and its derivatives (Hansen, 1959; Geertman and van Eck, 1995):

$$a_i = \sum_j o_j d_{ij}^{-\beta}$$

where a_i is the accessibility of location i; o_j is the attractiveness of opportunities at destination j; d_{ij} is the distance (or travel time) between locations i and j; and β is a calibrated "friction-of-distance" parameter. Outcome measures use actual travel behavior and interactions to quantify "realized accessibility" as a surrogate for accessibility.

Another issue is that of distinguishing between accessibility and *mobility* (Scott, 2000). Mobility-based measures simply quantify mobility or the physical ease of movement within a given environment. These measures include travel times or distance. Broader conceptualizations of accessibility treat mobility as only one component of a wider context for travel that includes the opportunities at travel destinations and the general costs (social, economic, political, psychological) of reaching those destinations (Handy, 1994).

Space-Time Accessibility

Accessibility measures involve implicit assumptions regarding what is being accessed, by whom, and how. Accessibility measures should be sensitive to the widely varying needs and resources of different social and demographic groups. The daily, weekly, and monthly activity schedules of individuals vary substantially by socioeconomic class, life cycle, culture, and gender roles (see Golledge and Stimson, 1997). Accessibility measures that are sensitive to different social and demographic contexts should incorporate the spatial and temporal constraints imposed by individuals' activity schedules and the ability to overcome these spatiotemporal constraint results.

Space-time accessibility measures are measures that incorporate constraints imposed by individuals' activities in space and time. Space-time accessibility measures can capture these constraints effectively (Kwan,

1998; Miller and Wu, 2000). A central concept in space-time accessibility measures is the *space-time prism* (Figure 3.7). This figure is an extension of the space-time path discussed in Chapter 2 (Figure 2.1). In this simple example, an individual is required to be at a specific location until a specified time and then return to that location at a later time (for example, a person who can leave the office during lunch but must return for the afternoon). Given this anchoring location, a time "budget" for travel and activity participation, and an assumed average travel velocity that is uniform across space, a three-dimensional space-time prism can be constructed. The interior of the prism is the *potential path space* (i.e., all locations in space and time that can be occupied by the space-time path during that discretionary period). The projection of the prism to the two-dimensional plane provides the *potential path area* (i.e., all locations in geographic space that the person can occupy during that discretionary period). Figure 3.7 is a simple illustration; the space-time prism can be

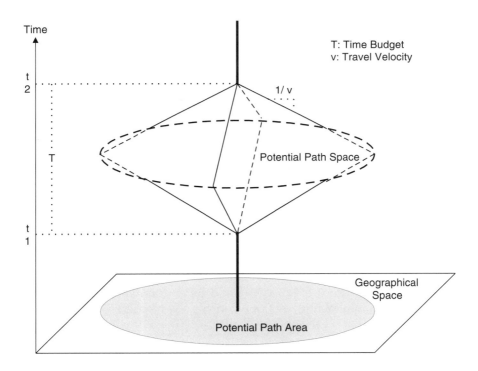

FIGURE 3.7 A space-time prism. SOURCE: Wu and Miller (in press).

more complex geometrically with noncoincident anchoring locations, different spatial metrics, and required activity time removed from the prism (see Burns, 1979).

The classical space-time prism assumption of a uniform travel velocity is a glaring oversimplification of more complex travel environments where travel velocities can vary by location (e.g., central city versus suburb, residential street versus highway) and time (e.g., peak hours versus non-peak hours). The greater availability of digital geographic data and the increased ability to process geographic information can allow one to relax this assumption when calculating and applying space-time prisms. One possibility is to use travel time data for transportation networks to construct network versions of the space-time prism. A simple algorithm based on the shortest-path procedure allows calculation of a network-based *potential path tree*: this shows all nodes in the network that are reachable given anchoring locations, a time budget, and travel times within the network (Miller, 1991). Behavioral constraints such as limited information can also be included (Kwan and Hong, 1998). Quantitative accessibility measures, such as constrained potential measures, can also be calculated using these and other network space-time prism measurements (Miller, 1999b; Miller and Wu, 2000).

Accessibility is an important component of livability, and more specifically of social equity as it relates to livability. However, in terms of analysis, accessibility is a complex function of distance, time, ease of mobility, and other factors. Space-time accessibility measures derived from time geography highlight the role of transportation technology in trading time for space but do not incorporate the role that communication and information technologies play in eliminating space for certain activities. Yet, even as these technologies permit more activities and information exchange in cyberspace, persistent inequalities in access to information technologies (often called the digital gap or divide) will create even wider differences in accessibility among social and demographic groups (Dodge and Kitchin, 2001). Researchers are extending the analyses of time geography to include communication and information technologies using time as a common metric to integrate geographic and cyberspace (see Adams, 1995, 2000; Kwan, 2000b; Shen, 2000). These analyses should create powerful, integrated measures of accessibility that capture the use of (or exclusion from) transportation and information technologies within the constraints dictated by activity schedules and locations.

Space-time perspective offers a powerful perspective for measuring accessibility at an individual level. Implementing this perspective in applied analysis requires data on individual space-time activities. In the past, collecting these data was prohibitively expensive, time-consuming, and fraught with errors. However, the increasing deployment of position-aware technologies, such as cell phones, wireless personal digital assistants, and global positioning system-enabled devices, is greatly lowering the cost and improving the accuracy of these data (see Smyth, 2001). Theories and tools for analyzing these data are also becoming increasingly available; for examples, consult the reference cited previously in this section as well as the edited volume by Frank, et al. (2001).

SUMMARY AND CONCLUSION

This chapter discusses spatial and temporal issues involved in measuring and analyzing livability. The discussion includes how to measure place-based indicators and how to measure accessibility, a complex phenomenon that conditions livability. Major conclusions and recommendations follow:

1. Many geographic boundaries are arbitrary and affect the collection of geographic data and the measurement of livability. Digital geographic data and GIS tools should be used to conduct sensitivity analyses of livability indicators with respect to boundary changes.
2. Many aggregate geographic units are arbitrary and create artificial effects in data collection and livability measurement with respect to spatial aggregation and zoning. Digital geographic data and GIS tools should be used to conduct sensitivity analyses of livability indicators with respect to changes in aggregation and zoning. Computational methods can also be used to form optimal spatial units for some measures.
3. Using only a place-based perspective may result in ecological fallacy and misrepresentation of livability differences across individuals. Using a people-based perspective where indicators are tracked with respect to individuals rather than locations is a useful complement. Both place-based and people-based perspectives are required to capture the full spectrum of livability and its variations.
4. Human settlement landscapes exhibit substantial and complex variability with respect to time as well as place. Recording livability data for a place only at one particular time can misrepresent urban and regional structure and processes. Livability should be analyzed over time as well as space at time scales varying from daily to weekly, monthly, yearly, and over multiple decades. This should be accomplished using both people-based and placed-based perspectives.
5. Livability data are often recorded or reported using incompatible spatial units. Appropriate spatial basis transfer methods should be used to integrate these data. The appropriate method depends on

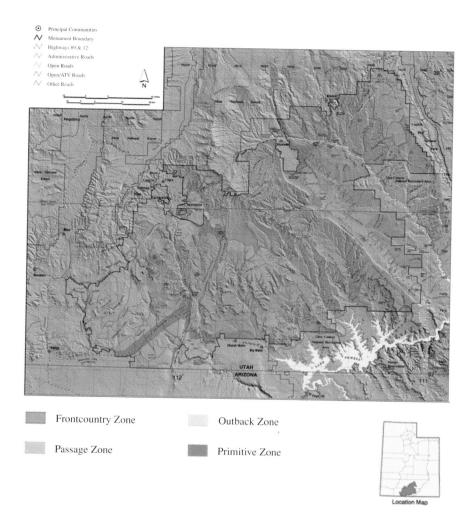

Frontcountry Zone   Outback Zone

Passage Zone   Primitive Zone

Location Map

PLATE 5 Grand Staircase-Escalante, Management Zones and Transportation System. The Frontcountry Zone (78, 056 acres) is intended to be the focal point for visitation by providing day use opportunities close to adjacent communities and to Highways 12 and 89. This zone would accommodate the primary interpretation, overlooks, trails, and associated facilities necessary to feature monument resources. The Passage Zone (38, 316 acres) includes secondary travel routes that receive use as throughways and recreation destinations. Rudimentary facilities necessary to protect resources, to educate visitors about monument resources, or for public safety would be provided. The Outback Zone (537,662 acres) is intended to provide an undeveloped primitive and self-directed visitor experience while

continued

accommodating motorized and mechanized access on designated routes. Facilities would be rare and provided only where essential for resource protection. The Primitive Zone (1,211,386 acres) provides an undeveloped, primitive, and self-directed visitor experience without motorized or mechanized access. Some administrative routes are included in the zone, which could allow very limited motorized access to authorized users. Facilities would be virtually nonexistent. Data were gathered from a variety of sources and integrated to provide a planning context. Data shown outside the Monument may not have been verified. The map represents available information and should not be interpreted to alter existing authorities or management responsibilities. SOURCE: Produced by Grand Staircase-Escalante National Monument (1999).

Kwan, M.-P. 2000a. Interactive geovisualization of activity-travel patterns using three-dimensional geographical information systems: A methodological exploration with a large data set. Transportation Research C: Emerging Technologies 8:185-203.

Kwan, M.-P. 2000b. Human extensibility and individual hybrid accessibility in space-time: A multiscale representation using GIS. Pp. 241-256 in D. G. Janelle and D. C. Hodge, eds., Information, Place and Cyberspace: Issues in Accessibility. Berlin: Springer

Kwan, M.-P., and X.-D. Hong. 1998. Network-based constraints-oriented choice set formation using GIS. Geographical Systems 5:139-162.

Martin, R. J. 1987. Some comments on correction techniques for boundary effects and missing value techniques. Geographical Analysis 19:273-282.

Mesev, V., P. Longley, and M. Batty. 1996. RS-GIS: Spatial distributions from remote imagery. Pp. 123-148 in P. Longley and M. Batty, eds., Spatial Analysis: Modeling in a GIS Environment. Cambridge, U.K.: GeoInformation International.

Miller, H. J. 1991. Modeling accessibility using space-time prism concepts within geographical information systems. International Journal of Geographical Information Systems 5:287-301.

Miller, H. J. 1999a. Potential contributions of spatial analysis to geographic information systems for transportation (GIS-T). Geographical Analysis 31:373-399.

Miller, H. J. 1999b. Measuring space-time accessibility benefits within transportation networks: Basic theory and computational methods. Geographical Analysis 31:187-212.

Miller, H. J., and Y.-H. Wu. 2000. GIS software for measuring space-time accessibility in transportation planning and analysis. GeoInformatica 4:141-159.

Monmonier, M. 1996. How to Lie with Maps, 2nd edition. Chicago: University of Chicago Press.

Openshaw, S. 1977. Optimal zoning systems for spatial interaction models. Environment and Planning A 9:169-184.

Openshaw, S. 1978. An empirical study of some zone-design criteria. Environment and Planning A 10:781-794.

Openshaw, S., and L. Rao. 1995. Algorithms for reengineering the 1991 census geography. Environment and Planning A 27:425-446.

Openshaw, S., and P. J. Taylor. 1979. A million or so correlation coefficients: Three experiments on the modifiable areal unit problem. Pp. 127-144 in N. Wrigley, ed., Statistical Applications in the Spatial Sciences. London: Pion.

Ord, J. K., and A. Getis. 1995. Local spatial autocorrelation statistics: Distributional issues and an application. Geographical Analysis 27:286-306.

Rogerson, P.A. 1990. Buffon's needle and the estimation of migration distances. Mathematical Population Studies 2:229-238.

Scott, L. M. 2000. Evaluating intra-metropolitan accessibility in the information age: Operational issues, objectives and implementation. Pp. 21-45 in D. G. Janelle and D. C. Hodge, eds., Information, Place and Cyberspace: Issues in Accessibility. Berlin: Springer.

Shen, Q. 2000. Transportation, telecommunications and the changing geography of opportunity. Urban Geography 20:334-355; reprinted on pp. 47-72 in D. G. Janelle and D. C. Hodge, eds., Information, Place and Cyberspace: Issues in Accessibility. Berlin: Springer.

Smyth, C. S. 2001. Mining mobile trajectories. In H. J. Miller and J. Han, eds., Geographic Data Mining and Knowledge Discovery. London: Taylor and Frances.

Taylor, P. J., and D. N. Parkes. 1975. A Kantian view of the city: A factorial ecology experiment in space and time. Environment and Planning A 7:671-688.

Theobald, D. 2001. Quantifying urban and rural sprawl using the sprawl index. Paper presented at the 97th annual meeting of the Association of American Geographers, New York, February 27-March 3.

van der Knaap, W. G. M. 1997. Analysis of time-space activity patterns in tourist recreation complexes: A GIS-oriented methodology. Pp. 283-311 in D. F. Ettema and H. J. P. Timmermans, eds., Activity-Based Approaches to Travel Analysis. Oxford, U.K.: Elsevier Science.

Wong, D., and C. Amrhein. 1996. Research on MAUP: Old wine in a new bottle or a real breakthrough? Geographical Systems 3:73-76.

Wong, D. W. S., and A. S. Fotheringham. 1990. Urban systems as examples of bounded chaos: Exploring the relationship between fractal dimension, rank-size and rural-to-urban migration. Geografiska Annaler 72B:89-99.

Wu, Y.-H., and H. J. Miller. Forthcoming. Computational tools for measuring space-time accessibility within transportation networks with dynamic flow. Journal of Transportation and Statistics.

National Capital, Traffic Circle, 1942, by Gluyas Williams. Courtesy of *New Yorker* magazine.

4

The Decision-Support Process

INTRODUCTION

This chapter focuses on the decision-support process for transportation, beginning with a look back to the antecedents of current practices in transportation planning and decision making. It then reviews the current process and concludes with recommendations on the "who, what, and why" of informed transportation decision making for livable communities.

An improved decision-support process—including both data and tools—will help focus attention on the real consequences of transportation investments within communities. Improved data will aid broader consideration of often narrowly defined transportation consequences—for example, better transit access to major attractions, enhanced goods movement, shorter travel times—and foster more insightful consideration of the socioeconomic, land use, and environmental factors that help shape a community's livability. These factors include mobility and equity consequences across locations within a region and across stakeholder groups; impacts on land use and development patterns and the consequences of those development patterns; the interaction of transportation operations with the natural and built environments, and impacts on sustainability; distribution of economic benefits and costs spatially and demographically; and consequences for community cohesiveness and character.

As communities, transportation planners, and decision makers have sharpened their understanding of the links between transportation and livability, the list of questions to be considered in making transportation choices has grown in length and complexity. These questions extend from the most basic (e.g., should we consider transportation improvements?), to highly detailed consideration of the interactions between transportation improvements and other valued community features, to the final decision on whether action is warranted based on the projected benefits, costs, and impacts. Such decisions impact the livability of communities and require large bodies of data, many of them crosscutting in nature, to adequately answer the questions and provide informed choices to decision makers.

CONTEXT OF CURRENT PRACTICES

Good transportation has long been recognized as an important element of a successful society—from the Roman roads, which helped unite an empire, to farm roads, which help bring products to market. Moreover, the physical development of a community has been shaped by the transportation technology that existed during each growth period, whether it was canoes, horsecars, or freeways.

The importance of transportation to the economy and society has given transportation decisions great significance and those who make them great power. The importance of the central government in transportation decisions was debated during the formative years of the United States, and transportation continues to be an important function of federal, state, and local governments. The transcontinental railroad was seen as an important factor in unifying the United States after the Civil War, and the Eisenhower Interstate Highway System in the 1950s reshaped population patterns and goods distribution to both a domestic and a world market.

This history would suggest the evolution of a highly sophisticated practice, beginning with the transportation studies of the 1950s in Detroit, Chicago, and other metropolitan areas, and concurrent with the early development of computers. For example, the algorithm needed to calculate the shortest path through a network or to estimate traffic flows was borrowed from early research on telephone networks. Once transportation planning moved beyond understanding current travel patterns (which could be estimated though travel surveys) into projections, data needs escalated quickly.

In his review of the history of transportation planning, Weiner points out that "through its evolutionary development, the urban transportation planning process has been called upon to address a continuous stream of new issues and concerns, methodological developments, advances in technology, and changing attitudes. The list of issues included safety, citizen involvement, preservation of parkland and natural areas, equal opportunity for disadvantaged persons, environmental concerns (particularly air quality), transportation for the elderly and handicapped, energy conservation, and the revitalization of urban centers" (Weiner, 1992).

This history also suggests the need for a highly responsive, collaborative decision-making process that is well attuned to livability factors. Such a process would reach beyond a confined view of transportation facility choices and embrace the ways in which these choices interact with valued community assets and impact livability. Instead, transportation planners and providers are often criticized as being impediments to the creation of more livable places and failing to look at transportation choices through the lens of livability. Much planning continues to be narrowly focused on transportation alone, particularly on highways, while concerns such as alternative ways to meet mobility needs, land use interactions, and environmental impacts are given less attention.

For several decades, urban planners have recognized that public investment projects in metropolitan regions must be considered within the regional context, not just with reference to the immediate project site. Public parklands, water supply, and sewer systems are several early examples of such metropolitan issues. In the transportation arena, parkway systems in cities such as Boston are early examples. In most of these cases, the metropolitan perspective derives significantly from the fact that sponsor agencies and decision makers have been municipal or regional entities.

In contrast, state departments of transportation have sponsored much of the major new public investment in transportation, predominantly highways, funded through the interstate highway system and other federal funding programs. One of the unintended consequences of this well-funded, highly focused, largely single-purpose effort has been a disconnect in planning these investments between the projects and the local and regional contexts within which they set. They have been designed and implemented with little sense of the surrounding place and little focus on how they affect the livability of the host community beyond a narrowly defined transportation function.

The National Environmental Policy Act (NEPA) and associated regulations from federal transportation agencies sought to require consideration of the environmental interactions and impacts of such federally funded public investments. More recently, the Intermodal Surface Transportation Efficiency Act (ISTEA) focused on the need to explicitly consider and analyze major transportation investments in a metropolitan region context, based on sound planning principles.

Current Transportation Planning Process

The traditional transportation planning process has four steps and is carried out at local, regional, and statewide levels. First, goals and objectives are developed. These often are in the form of level of service standards or other desirable operating conditions for the transportation system. These goals and objectives should be based on community values and cover such topics as structural condition, congestion levels, safety, alternative modes, and other transportation outcomes.

The second step is determining system deficiencies based on the goals and objectives. Often, transportation demand models are used to determine where current and future congestion deficiencies exist. Traditional models assume current and future land use patterns as a given from local comprehensive plans, and forecast traffic conditions given those patterns of growth. Land use can also be a variable, since land use patterns affect modal travel and travel patterns, and since transportation facilities have a feedback effect on land use.

The third step is alternatives analysis, in which different approaches to fixing deficiencies are examined. Increasingly, alternatives analysis examines multiple modes of transportation (e.g., simultaneous access to highways, bicycle paths, and mass transit) as possible solutions. Travel demand models are also used to evaluate how alternatives perform on a system level.

The final step is selection of a preferred alternative. This preferred alternative is usually a result of compromise among competing interests and often includes a mix of modal components that work together to address the deficiency.

Transportation models have been developed to predict the likely origins and destinations of trips and the likely use of different modes, based on projections of where people would live, work, and play. Just like livability, assessing travel requires data on both people and places. Such information was generally not available in the 1960s (and frequently is not available today), so transportation planners often had to create the data for themselves. As a result, decision-support tools were not designed for the diverse stakeholders involved in livability planning. They were instead developed as inputs to transportation models at different geographic scales than were common for public planning data.

Long-Range Planning

Planning for transportation is typically large scale and long term, whether at the statewide or local level, and it requires project development (i.e., project-specific planning). Long-term plans are developed by state departments of transportation or, for major metropolitan areas, by metropolitan planning organization (MPOs). Project planning can occur at the local scale or, with very large projects, for large corridors or sectors of a region; and they can be sponsored by a state department of transportation, the MPO, or a local unit of government—a municipality or county—depending on the project.

Long-range plans typically have a 20- or 30-year time horizon and build on the area's long-term vision, as well as long-term projections of population, economic development, and transportation needs. They also include a short-term element, in which specific transportation improvements are programmed for each of the coming years—either a statewide transportation improvement program or the MPO's transportation improvement program, including specific projects.

Project Planning

Project planning is the process by which a proposal for a specific transportation improvement is assessed. In the process of planning a federally funded project, major decisions focus around these questions:

- Is the solution a project (such as building a trolley line) or non-project solution (such as changing the timing of signals to improve traffic flows and give buses and emergency vehicles priority at intersections)?
- Will the project be likely to have any significant impacts?

The answer to these questions determines the types of analyses that will be required to comply with NEPA requirements. If the answers are uncertain, an assessment is performed to determine whether there will be significant impacts. If so, draft and final environmental impact statements are required, followed by a record of decision. The Federal Highway Administration (FHWA) and the Federal Transit Administration (FTA) have issued regulations to guide transportation agencies on complying with NEPA in assessing transportation improvements.

Changes in the Transportation Planning Process

Meyer (1999) suggests that two issues in particular will strongly characterize the next period of planning: the first is technology applications in the broadest sense (such as Geographic Information Systems [GISs]), and the second is growing awareness of sustainable development. GIS and visualization are just beginning to be used widely; technical engineering standards, design standards, and mathematical models are more commonly used. Benchmark measures typically focus on the physical infrastructure. An excellent example of a different approach is the Aurora Partnership, a public-private collaboration to stimulate the development of decision-support tools, services, and systems and the application of spatial data for natural resource and environmental management (http://aurorapartnership.org). It seeks to address the needs of policy makers, land and resource managers, and county and community leaders. The four principles of the Aurora Partnership, formed in 1998, are the following:

1. Support existing and new partnerships at local, regional, and national levels.
2. Adopt a perspective of place-based management incorporating other user needs in addition to those associated with natural resources and the environment.
3. Focus on decision processes and stakeholder involvement as well as technology and software.
4. Provide a national forum for the exchange of decision-support knowledge.

Although the practice of transportation planning is technically sophisticated, it tends to be focused on travel and traffic outputs and does not pay much attention to sustainability and livability indicators. Most of the standard tools are not easy to use and require special training and experience available only to the most technically sophisticated agencies.

Since the 1980s, decision makers, planners, and community members have stressed the importance of a multimodal and intermodal perspective on transportation. Multimodal refers to the inclusion of many modes—highway, transit, railroad, walking, bicycle, and so forth—in deciding how best to meet mobility and access needs. Intermodal refers to the links between modes—a bus-rail station or cargo carried on a ship and then a truck—and the nature of most trips, whether by people or goods.

Decisions based on such modal considerations require integrated databases, which capture both the functional aspects of the modes and how they relate to one another and the relationship between the choice of modes and impacts of transportation investment and service decisions on livability. Indeed, many of the arguments related to the choice of one mode over another are tied directly to crosscutting considerations of livability. For instance, the choice of a highway for a corridor instead of public transit will entail much more fuel consumption and associated environmental impacts, and the highway may well contribute to exurbanization and sprawl. However, the highway choice will provide better service for goods movement, along with associated economic benefits, and may well enhance personal choice and mobility for door-to-door auto trips.

By way of an intermodal example, the decision on whether to invest in a new intermodal ship-truck-rail terminal will include consideration of environmental, economic, land use, and other impacts on the immediate and surrounding areas, in addition to more narrow considerations of transportation functions and economies of different movement patterns between the modes. Thus, it is impossible to take a broad perspective across and among transportation modes without considering livability impacts and options.

Transportation plans are best made in the broad context of the long-term goals of the community, state, or region. This long-term vision must include thinking about factors such as projected population growth, economic change, transportation needs and maintenance requirements, and potential impacts of alternatives on natural and human environments.

Transportation decisions involve a great breadth of issues. Major transportation projects are undertaken for a variety of purposes, including safety improvement, reduction in congestion, and promotion of economic development. Other reasons include national defense and counter-cyclical investments to jump-start a slow economy. However, with sufficient support at the federal level, livability could be introduced as one of the specific items to be addressed in federally funded transportation planning. It is important to change the attitudes of participants to make livability an important goal.

Such a change may be occurring already. A movement known as "context-sensitive design" aspires to lessen the negative effects of routing streets and highways through living areas and to foster the reestablishment of a community sense of place. According to Thomas Warne, past president of the American Association of State Highway and Transportation Officials, ". . . highway projects can be designed with imagination, creativity, and collaboration to preserve and enhance the character and quality of community without sacrificing transportation mobility and safety." Five "lead states" (Connecticut, Kentucky, Maryland, Minnesota, and Utah) are pressing this initiative with support from the FHWA (Gavin, 2000). As part of the 1991 ISTEA, all metropolitan planning in the United States was required to address a set of 15 factors, grouped under three categories: (1) mobility and access, (2) system performance and preservation, and (3) environment and quality of life. (See Box 4.1, which includes examples of data that should be used to assess livability.) Despite the fact that this mandate was dropped in the 1997 transportation legislation (known as the Transportation Equity Act for the 21st Century [TEA-21]), these factors represent important considerations in metropolitan

BOX 4.1
Metropolitan Planning Factors Assessing Impacts on Livability

Mobility and Access for People and Goods

Factor 1. Effects of all transportation projects (e.g., cumulative impact of the system on land use and development patterns, open space and natural area degradation, sprawl, housing affordability, and access of people in different economic strata to jobs)

Factor 2. International border crossings and the promotion of access to critical areas and activities (e.g., extent to which links with border crossings enhance regional and national economic competitiveness, distribution of economic benefits by industry and job sector, and impacts on employment and job creation by industry sector and location)

Factor 3. Road connectivity from inside to outside metropolitan areas (e.g., impacts of connectivity on local and regional growth and development plans, improved access to jobs by population and income sectors, impacts on traditionally underserved segment of the population, and impacts of connectivity on increased pressure for development in environmentally sensitive areas)

Factor 4. Enhancement of efficient freight movement (e.g., impacts on location and distribution of freight-related industries, contribution to employment and job creation for underemployed sectors of the population, and noise and other impacts on sensitive environmental resources)

Factor 5. Expansion and enhancement of transit services and use (e.g., improved access to education and jobs for low-income, female-headed, and autoless households; increased mode share by geographic area for transit; and level of reduction in environmental impacts resulting from shifts to transit from auto and single-occupant vehicle trips [for peak and off-peak periods])

System Performance and Preservation

Factor 6. Congestion relief and prevention (e.g., extent to which congestion relief measures promote efficient energy use and energy savings; impacts of congestion relief and prevention on economic productivity in the movement of people and goods)

Factor 7. Preservation and efficient use of existing transportation facilities (e.g., economic impacts, by sector, from transportation to asset protection, potential shift of resources from capital to maintenance expenditures, and impacts on business sectors and job classifications)

transportation planning, and they should be incorporated in the planning process at an early stage. The relevance of each factor will of course vary depending on local circumstances, as will the manner in which transportation planners consider and analyze these factors. However, it is important that the factors be given explicit and appropriate consideration. The

Factor 8. Transportation needs identified through the implementation of management systems (e.g., needs by demographic and economic sector, by location and transportation mode; extent to which meeting needs will promote more equitable distribution of transportation benefits and costs by population sector)

Factor 9. Preservation of rights-of-way (e.g., extent to which preservation of rights-of-way reduces the impacts of development and exurbanization; impacts of preserved rights-of-way on movement patterns of wildlife and preservation of plant communities)

Factor 10. Use of life cycle costs in the design and engineering of bridges (e.g., extent to which life cycle costing presents a more full accounting of the total costs of the investment, including the distribution of costs over time, by location, and by economic sector)

Environment and Quality of Life

Factor 11. Overall social, economic, energy, and environmental effects of transportation decisions (e.g., crosscutting impacts of the transportation program; extent to which transportation investments stimulate positive economic development, protect environmental resources, and are consistent with regional land use and development goals; also, trade-offs between economic benefits and costs and land use or development and environmental benefits and costs)

Factor 12. Consistency of planning with energy conservation measures (e.g., changes in transportation energy consumption by household income, including progressive or regressive impacts of transportation energy taxes by income level and impacts of changes in energy consumption on air quality)

Factor 13. Relationships between transportation and short- and long-term land use planning (e.g., impacts on short-term housing costs, by income group according to race and location, and impacts on long-term housing and development patterns, particularly in terms of development concentration and transit-supportive development)

Factor 14. Programming of expenditures on transportation enhancement activities (e.g., distribution of enhancement activities by location, measured by socioeconomic characteristics of neighborhoods surrounding the location)

Factor 15. Capital investments that increase transit system security (e.g., impacts of increased security and lower crime on perceived community livability)

FHWA and the FTA recognize the complexities involved in the consideration and analysis of some of these factors, and have established general guidelines with respect to consideration and analysis of the 15 factors. Their consideration may also be a part of the public involvement process, a major investment study (MIS), or adjustments to management systems implementation, all of which are required in the metropolitan planning process. Nonetheless, these agencies have established general guidelines with respect to the consideration and analysis of the 15 factors.

Decision Process Framework

Although analysts may be uncomfortable dealing with conflicting goals, they are a fact of life. People prefer not to choose between, say, a good economy and a healthy environment or a suburban environment and free-flowing roads. They want both livability and affordability. These conflicting desires create a potential dilemma for those making transportation decisions. For example, at what point does mobility degrade rather than enhance livability? More importantly, how will that decision be made and by whom? At some point, these questions must be addressed.

The decision-making process includes all stages of the decision from problem definition, to alternative selection, to implementation and evaluation. Key components are identification and definition of the problem; formulation and evaluation of alternative courses of action; and selection, implementation, and evaluation of the solution. Stakeholders include those who might be affected or served by the decision, as well as those advising decision makers of their viewpoints.

Meyer and Miller (2001) stress the complexity of the transportation planning process resulting, in part, from the varied perspectives and purposes of the people involved in the process (see Box 4.2 for discussion). In addition, transportation decisions must take a future perspective on outcomes and stakeholder needs. Boulding (1974) suggested these important considerations:

> Transportation planning must be seen as an integral part of a much wider process of decision making. Too often in the past transportation solutions have been seen as the only way to resolve transportation problems . . . transportation must be seen as part of the land-use planning and development process which requires an integrated approach to analysis and a clear vision of the type of city and society in which we wish to live.

A decision-oriented approach to urban transportation planning should focus on the information needs of interested decision makers and should recognize the often limited capability of individuals unfamiliar with technical analysis to interpret the information produced. Planning should provide not only the information *desired* by decision makers, but also the information *needed* to provide a more complete understanding of the problem and of the implications of different solutions.

BOX 4.2
Decision Considerations

The world moves into the future as a result of decisions (or lack of decisions), not as a result of careful planning. However, planning can be effective if it provides useful information to those who must make decisions. In this case, it must provide not only information that is desired by decision makers, but also information that illuminates the short- and long-term consequences of alternative choices.

Decision making involves two major elements: (1) an agenda consisting of alternative images of the future, along with some concept of the relationship between present action and future societal directions, and (2) a valuation scheme that outlines preferences for the characteristics of likely decision outcomes. In the case of urban transportation, this valuation scheme is often intricately tied to societal values and goals, expressed in the political decision-making process.

Evaluations and decisions are influenced by the degree of uncertainty associated with expected consequences. Decisions regarding future actions are based on implicit and explicit assumptions about the likely consequences of alternative decisions and the future state of the urban area in which the decisions will be implemented. Thus, the greater the degree of uncertainty associated with these assumptions, the higher is the value that should be placed on decisions that leave future options open. The value of an option—a fundamental concept from modern economic and financial theory—is relevant here. In addition to the obvious applications in the theory of financial options, the value of an option has also been the subject of extensive literature on "real options" in business investment (Dixit and Pindyck, 1994; Copeland and Antikarov, 2001) and on the importance of recognizing irreversibilities in evaluating the costs and benefits of development that threatens ecological resources (Fisher et al., 1972).

The products of planning should be designed to increase the chance of making better decisions. Planning should examine a wide range of agendas, the values and objectives underlying the current decision, past decisions that were not considered to be effective, failures of past predictions, and early warnings that the assumed state of the future is changing.

The result of planning involves some form of communication with decision makers. The products of planning are only a small part of the information input. To increase the usefulness of this planning information, planning products and processes should reflect the substantive and information-understanding requirements of the individuals who will use these products, including information about livability.

SOURCE: Meyer and Miller (2001).

Decisions Resolve Conflicting Ideas

Tension between technical and political decisions often contributes to transportation-related conflict. One contributing factor is that the locus of decision-making control is often not the same as the area of impact. Much of the funding for transportation projects, for example, especially highway spending, is controlled by state transportation agencies, while impacts, both positive and negative, fall on local jurisdictions who often have little practical say in the decisions. Transit and airport operations tend to be more solidly grounded in local issues because such planning involves greater elements of local control. At the other end of the spectrum, decisions involving real estate development, which affect future travel needs, are local, with state transportation agencies having little influence.

Major transportation facilities have a long life span, justifying the care and planning invested in such projects; however, elected officials and citizens often have a much shorter time perspective. Economic considerations may accelerate the transportation decision-making process in order to serve the changing needs of business and public facilities. However, quick decisions often impede important plans and procedures. Long-range planning requires extensive and time-consuming dialogue among politicians, professionals, and the public. Many players have a role to play in the process.

In many urban areas, the MPO is designated to sort out any conflicts. Lacking formal authority over local governments however, this organization generally serves as a clearinghouse, with most of the key decisions made elsewhere. However, many agencies and groups are involved in decision making at the metropolitan level, so a regional perspective is helpful in seeing how these many actors and activities interact.

Regional Basis for Decision Making

It is the regional nature of transportation demand that dictates a broad view of services. Local officials generally shape the spatial form of the region; transportation and utility providers build the infrastructure; and developers build the real estate needed to accommodate or anticipate growth. (Developers include a wide variety of corporate and institutional property owners and users.) An important challenge is to develop a vision so compelling and a consensus so strong that it carries across political agendas.

Business locations and the movement of goods are often scattered across a market area, drawing on the need for regional roads, transit, water, and utility networks. Still, effective and continuing regional cooperation remains uncommon. Local governments often compete for new businesses to help the tax base or, as it is sometimes called, the "ratables race." They may also strive for the best schools or the most state revenues.

Clearly, families and businesses try to select locations where services meet their needs. Enabling such choice is important. This idea is expressed in the famous Tiebout Model showing the interaction between household and business location, on the one hand, and local governmental decision making, on the other (Tiebout, 1956). This model has inspired an enormous amount of literature. It is controversial not only as a description of the real-world tax and service competition by local governments, but also in its implications that real-world processes produce "optimal" results. Nevertheless, the basic concept of competition among these factors clearly has a substantial measure of truth. (For extensive discussions, see Atkinson and Stiglitz, 1980, Ch. 17, and various essays in Zodrow, 1983.)

Although it is difficult to gain consensus about a region, it is essential for addressing regional issues such as transportation. Some regional agencies, as well as private citizens' organizations, have been influential in establishing a regional vision, which always has a spatial dimension and broad-based perspective. This vision includes a mix of urban and rural, high-density and low-density, and contiguous and noncontiguous development, which can help residents and businesses develop a place-based vision. While a regional vision is eventually needed, it must be built up from community-level images. In Charlottesville, Virginia, for example, a clear description of potential development patterns (moderate-density housing or town centers, for example) is translated into the types of projects that builders will build and lenders will finance (see Box 1.4).

The case study of the planning of I-69 in Box 4.3 provides an example of integrated planning on a regional basis. It describes the planning for a highway incorporating environmental concerns, from the start rather than at the end, in the form of an environmental impact statement.

Actors in Transportation Decision Making

In many decisions, the most important question is, Who's in charge? There are many major groups involved in transportation-related decisions—for example, transportation providers, local officials, and developers. Another important stakeholder group is citizens, who have the power to stop most controversial projects. The key is to engage all groups, up front, in a vision that they can all support.

Those who make decisions on transportation investments include both elected and appointed public officials and boards, along with staff members of transportation agencies. While much of the focus is on major decisions that come at the end of the planning process—for example, by the chief executive of a state department of transportation to construct a new highway or by the public transportation agency to expand a bus terminal—many important decisions are made in the course of the transportation planning and analysis process.

Although often perceived as routine or as part of the day-to-day practice of transportation planners and engineers, such decisions can have a

BOX 4.3
The Mississippi Delta: An Ecological Framework:
U.S. EPA—Planning and Analysis Branch, Spring 2001

In August 2000, the Federal Highway Administration, U.S. Environmental Protection Agency (EPA), and U.S. Forest Service (USFS) agreed to be the lead agencies in a cooperative information-gathering effort regarding the natural resources of the Mississippi Delta region. This effort was intended to serve a variety of resource protection programs in the delta area, but was to be applied specifically to the pre-planning phases of a new highway slated to run through the Mississippi Delta: I-69.

The I-69 project was designated by Congress in 1991 as a high-priority corridor in ISTEA, connecting border crossings with Canada and Mexico and linking to the highway networks of these North American Free Trade Agreement (NAFTA) trading partners. The corridor has been referred to as a "North American trade route," filling a significant gap in the transportation system, serving increased traffic resulting from NAFTA, and supporting economic competitiveness. Although the broad corridor for the project is defined, the specific location has not been determined. The analyses now under way will assess alternative locations, their impacts, and mitigation measures before a final decision is made on the location of the highway.

This process is exemplary as a transportation planning effort in that environmental issues were addressed from the beginning, rather than after the fact with an environmental impact statement or a postdevelopment remediation. All available ecological data were collected from public and private agencies throughout the delta, in order to develop a model known as the "ecological framework," which was used as a pre-planning decision-support model for environmental mitigation and protection.

Recognizing that successful protection of natural resources requires more than "spot" conservation of isolated areas, this framework attempts to identify not only highly valuable and sensitive ecological areas, but also the links between them. One of the greatest threats to the environment is the loss of ecosystem function due to fragmentation of protected areas. Roads, agriculture, and other development often lead to the cutting up of natural systems into smaller and smaller segments. Large, contiguous tracts of natural land are required not only for species habitat range, such as migratory birds or black bears, but also for healthy ecosystem function. Many ecological processes, such as water filtration and functional evolution require large areas of land, often spanning multiple land cover types. Viable landscape linkages are needed to connect these areas so that ecological processes and healthy functioning of the land are preserved. These linkages are also helpful in adding to the legibility of the regional-scale landscape (as discussed in Chapter 2).

The Mississippi Delta Ecological Framework is being developed to identify areas of high ecological value and their best potential linkages. In addition, the model will identify potential mitigation and restoration sites. Identifying these areas early on may greatly expedite permit, mitigation, and funding procedures.

Ecological Framework Methodology

Common goals and objectives were set, and roles were determined through cross-agency and organization partnerships. The objective was to compile a common data-

continued

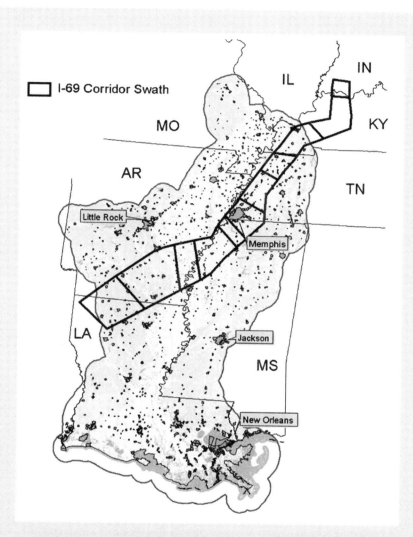

(A) Delta Initiative; Lower Mississippi Delta study area; potential I-69 corridor swath representation. SOURCE: LANDSAT 7 land cover imagery, 1992-1993. Image compiled by U.S. EPA Region IV.

continued

BOX 4.3 Continued

base and model to highlight priority ecological areas of the delta. The land areas were divided into several categories, including priority ecological areas, secondary ecological areas, potential ecological restoration areas, and links.

Priority ecological areas were used in the analysis to create hubs, analyzed by size, contiguousness, proximity to roads or urban areas, and compatible land cover. Data included urban areas, black bear habitat in known or potential occupied ranges of 10,000 acres or more, road-free areas of more than 5,000 acres, bird conservation areas, publicly managed lands, wetland reserve areas, reforestation areas, and habitat diversity areas. Secondary ecological areas were determined using data from potential bird conservation areas, potential black bear habitats, significant riparian areas, and road-free areas.

Potential ecological restoration areas were determined by measuring areas with high potential for reforestation, secondary ecological areas near or surrounded by agriculture, and smaller secondary ecological areas that could be linked to form larger units.

The links of least ecological cost—natural land cover areas—run between the priority ecological areas and function as ecological corridors. The understanding of these ecologically important areas and the linkages between them allows the appropriate staff at EPA, the U.S. Department of Transportation, TEA-21, and the FWHA to integrate these findings into their mitigation and transportation planning processes.

SOURCE: Stacy Fehlenberg, EPA, personal communication, 2001.

profound impact on the livability of communities. Deciding what data to include and exclude in long-range planning, assumptions made in the modeling of travel demand and population projections of the need for a project and the definition of its purpose, decisions on corridors and modal alternatives necessary to meet perceived mobility needs, what criteria and performance measures are selected for screening and analysis, and the inclusiveness and extent of meaningful community interaction in public participation programs—these are all "in-process" decisions that clearly shape the outcomes of planning and the range of choices made available to decision makers.

Better data related to livability would help to inform these in-process decisions and make the planning process more reflective of the real impact of transportation investments on communities. Further, an improved planning process provides the potential for improved decision making, not only because it yields a more complete body of information for decision makers, but also because this body of information will be available to individuals, stakeholder organizations, and public officials from communities potentially impacted by such decisions.

Individuals and groups may be excluded from the decision-making process by agenda setting that expressly or inadvertently makes the impacts of decision making a foregone conclusion prior to the process of discussing and agreeing upon data sources and information needs (Innes, 1996). Judith Innes (1996) discusses "communicative planning" and practices that draw on the work of Jurgen Habermas (Habermas, 1984, 1987). She makes three main points:

1. Communicative practice must be embedded in institutions and practices rather than being applied in a particular case by a scientist or planner interested in involving the public in the decision-making process.
2. The process by which information is produced and useful or necessary data for the decision are chosen (agreed upon) is crucial.
3. Many types of information may count, not just objective or formal information.

The third point refers to the choice of indicators that will be used to measure the effects of a decision or the success or failure of an intervention. Both qualitative and quantitative measures are important in the overall decision process.

Role of Public Involvement in the Decision Process

Strong public involvement is essential for sound transportation decision making. Just as definitions of what livability means in real communities derive from the perceptions and aspirations of their members, so must good decisions on transportation investments build on the wants and needs of the community and its perceptions of the desirability of investment options, including the no-build alternative. Clearly, this is a great challenge for transportation planners and decision makers, because various stakeholder groups in a community may have competing interests and different perceptions of the benefits and costs of a plan, especially if the distribution of benefits and costs leads to a disproportionate impact on one segment of the community or region. In fact, recent attention to environmental justice in transportation stems from concern over the potentially inequitable distribution of the benefits, impacts, and costs of transportation across population groups within the community. In addition to the technical assessment of these distributional effects, it is important to seek out and involve traditionally underserved members of the community as transportation services and facilities are planned.

The following are some of the key principles for strong public involvement of all stakeholders:

- Participation extends from the very start of planning through all decision points.
- Participants are involved in determining the involvement program that best fits their community, including its style and members' needs.
- A full range of interested and affected stakeholders is involved, including traditionally underinvolved and underserved segments.
- Programs are accessible in various locations, languages, and alternate viewpoints in order to allow participation by all community members.
- There is a mix of written, verbal, visual, graphic, and in-person techniques for community information, education, and involvement.
- Information is timely, complete, unbiased, and understandable to laypeople.
- Participants understand the process, timing, and people involved in decision making; and public involvement and inclusion efforts are particularly extensive around major decision points.
- The community is informed of major decisions, such as how its input was used (or not) and what will happen next.

When public involvement programs are developed with these principles in mind, both participants and decision makers benefit from a structured process for collaborative decision making that fosters open consideration of the trade-offs and consequences of decision choices. Within such a process, decision-support tools can further clarify and aid decision making.

Role of Decision-Support Tools

Nyerges (2001) identified eight types of systems for decision support (see Box 4.4). Nyerges argues that all eight system types make significant contributions to sound decision making by individual groups. Items e, f, and h (i.e., choice models, structured-group process techniques, analytical reasoning methods) are especially useful in comparing different solutions and achieving consensus across various groups. Software has been developed to support each of these eight functions, although no single product is capable of addressing all of these tasks. Sound software exists

---

BOX 4.4
Role of Tools in Decision Support

Level 1: Basic Information Handling Support
(a) Data management and access (e.g., storage, retrieval, and organization of spatial data and information using stand-alone or distributed database management system support)
(b) Visual aids (e.g., shared displays of charts, tables, maps, diagrams, matrix and/or other representational formats)
(c) Group collaboration support (e.g., idea generation, collection, and compilation; anonymous input of ideas, along with the pooling and display of textual ideas; electronic voting; electronic white boards; computer conferencing; and large-screen displays)

Level 2: Decision Analysis Support
(d) Phenomenon models (e.g., interlinkage indicator models, site suitability models, location-allocation optimization models, and dynamic simulation models)
(e) Choice models (e.g., option preference ranking lists based on pairwise comparison, multiple-criteria decision models, preference sensitivity modeling, and Bayesian decision models)
(f) Structured-group process techniques (e.g., brainstorming, Delphi, modified Delphi, and technology of participation)

Level 3: Group Reasoning Support
(g) Judgment refinement amplification techniques (e.g., the specific contribution of criteria to project options, sensitivity analysis, and social judgment analysis)
(h) Analytical reasoning methods (e.g., using mathematical programming or expert systems guided by automatic mediation, parliamentary procedure, or Robert's Rules of Order) that identify patterns in a reasoning process

---

SOURCE: Nyerges (2001).

---

for addressing a and b (i.e., data management and access, and visual aids), but the question remains whether any of these computer-based decision-support tools are adequate for comparative purposes.

Table 4.1 presents a summary of what Nyerges terms "Micro, Decision Strategy Activities"—the basic steps that are undertaken in any decision process—in the first column, and "Macro, Decision Strategy Phases" in the next three columns. The cells highlight helpful decision-support tools when carrying out different activities within different phases of the decision-making process.

TABLE 4.1 Micro, Decision Strategy Activities

Micro, Decision Strategy Activities	Macro, Decision Strategy Phases		
	Intelligence[a]	Design[b]	Choice[c]
Gather	Participant input on values, goal, and objectives using information and structured-group process.	Data using information management and phenomenon models to generate options	Values, criteria, and feasible decision options using group collaboration support methods
Organize	Goals and objectives using visual aids, group collaboration support, and structured-group process	An approach to decision option generation using structured-group process techniques and models	Values, criteria, and feasible decision options using choice models and structured-group process techniques
Select	Criteria to be used in decision process using group collaboration support methods	Decision options from outcomes generated by structured-group process techniques and models	Goal and consensus achieving decision options using choice models and structured-group process techniques
Review-approve	Criteria, resources, constraints, and standards using group collaboration support methods	Decision options and identification of feasible options using information management and choice models	Recommendations of decision options using judgment refinement techniques

[a]About values, objectives, and criteria.
[b]Of a feasible option set.
[c]About decision options.
SOURCE: Nyerges (2001).

Information Needs of Decision Makers

To make responsive, responsible decisions on potential transportation investments, decision makers need information such as that outlined in the 15 metropolitan planning factors in Box 4.1. This information can then be used to answer questions such as those that follow, for long-range plans and projects. These questions are not new. Rather, they are answered using more inclusive, crosscutting information that results from posing the questions within the context of decision making for livability, and then conducting the planning analyses with that broader information. These questions reflect the types of analyses that should be performed during the course of planning, and also correspond broadly to various stages in the planning and decision-making process. In addition to such analyses, close consultation with the public is an essential part of a sound planning and decision-making process. For long-range plans, the following questions are applicable:

- What is the geographic and temporal scope of the plan?
- Who was involved in developing the plan? In particular, was there significant, extensive, inclusive public involvement, and to what extent does the plan reflect the input of community participants, from individuals to interest groups, to elected and appointed officials, and including traditionally underrepresented and underserved members of the community?
- What is the region's vision for its future, and to what extent does this plan incorporate the goals and desired outcomes of the plan?
- What are projected demographic, economic, and other significant regional trends (including multiple states when this broader regional scale is relevant), and how realistic are the projections?
- Are all the relevant components and features of the community included in the plan (e.g., land use and development, open space and other environmental assets, housing, education, major community facilities)?
- To what extent does the long-range transportation plan relate coherently to other major plans, goals, community components, and features of the area?
- Are alternative ways of achieving the goals of the plan assessed?
- Are potential costs, benefits, impacts, and mitigation measures included in the plan, at a level of detail appropriate to long-range planning (versus project development)?
- Is livability explicitly addressed in the plan, including the following: a community-based definition, a discussion of the relationship of the transportation plan to community livability, and the use of crosscutting indicators expressing the impacts of the plan on livability?

For project planning, decision makers should document the following:

- the purpose of and need for the project;
- the goals of the project and relevant evaluation criteria;

- the project area, including relevant surrounding areas in the region and transportation system;
- comments from stakeholders about the desirability and impacts of the project (both positive and negative); documentation of the public participation program—its extent, components, and assessment of efforts to include the full range of project stakeholders, including traditionally underrepresented and underserved constituencies;
- alternatives that have been considered, those maintained and dismissed, and the rationale behind them;
- a statement about the trade-offs between different alternative ways to meet the need versus the likely impacts: Is a "no build" decision better than any build-implement choices?
- analyses performed and the results;
- a full accounting of the costs, benefits, and impacts of the project, including how impacts will be mitigated;
- the distribution of impacts, both positive and negative, spatially and among different subsets of the population: What primary and secondary impacts will result? Are there ripple effects through the transportation system that bring about other consequences? Are there similar ripple effects economically, socially, and environmentally?
- explicit consideration of the impacts of the project on the livability of the community, as defined by its members, and the extent to which crosscutting indicators of livability are included in the assessment of project consequences;
- relevant legislative and regulatory requirements and how they have been addressed in developing and evaluating the project; and
- the final conclusions—on balance, across these many interacting factors, what is the best choice, and what are the implications of that choice in the short and long term?

Information for decision makers, indeed, for all process participants, must be accurate, complete, timely, and expressed in terms that are understandable to laypeople. The information also has to be meaningful; that is, it must be sufficiently comprehensive to capture the range of interactions involved in the proposed plan or project with the surrounding community and the transportation system of which it is a part; and it must shed light on noteworthy differences between decision alternatives.

These interactions and the resulting impacts must include the kinds of data and crosscutting indicators that help explain what the consequences of the project or plan are in terms of community livability. The Government Accounting Standards Board (GASB) issued Statement 34 in 1999, which includes new accounting standards on the presentation of all assets and liabilities (including infrastructure) on the public balance sheet. In the short run, implementation of GASB 34 is putting a strain on public agencies, but in the long run it will produce new information about the magnitude and cost of transportation and infrastructure investments for all public entities. Implementation of GASB 34 reporting requirements will be easier for public agencies that have already documented their infrastructure using Geographic Information Systems.

CONCLUSIONS

Transportation decision making must be part of an integrated approach that reflects broad consideration of the relationship of transportation to achieving a community's vision of livability. The overall decision process is complex, involving a variety of decision-support tools, a potentially large and wide-ranging body of relevant information, and diverse participants. A decision-oriented approach to transportation planning should focus on the information needs of decision makers. As discussed throughout this report, the information needed for decision making that leads to livable communities often includes what we consider spatial data: for example, data about the location of resources such as hospitals or data about the relationship between one place and another, including the public transportation links between a city and its suburbs. The needed information is comprised of multidimensional social or economic data (e.g., children under age 5, per household, environmental or historical data such as location of toxic waste sites). Accordingly, it is important to recognize the limited experience of many decision makers with the kind of synthetic and technical analyses required to interpret and use the existing data.

The regional context of transportation decisions is important because of links between transportation, land use, and economic development at the regional scale. The history of transportation planning suggests the need for a highly responsive decision-making process, well attuned to recent interest in livability. Various tools contribute to sound decision making through supporting the basic handling of information, decision analysis, and group reasoning (Nyerges, 2001) and helping people to overcome their lack of familiarity with data and data analysis. Geographic information tools and visualization can also support the decision process. In particular, the following can improve the transportation decision-support process:

- working actively and collaboratively with the community from the very start of transportation planning, incorporating the community's definitions of livability in framing the issues and needs to be addressed in planning;

- conducting transportation planning—whether for a regional system or facility or a local project—within the regional context and relating issues, needs, and choices to that larger regional context;
- developing transportation plans within the context of long-term community and regional goals, including consideration of population and economic growth, land use and development, transportation access and mobility needs, and potential impacts on the natural and built environments;
- following the principles of context-sensitive design in developing transportation plans, particularly through collaboration with community members, consideration of the fit between facilities and services in the local context, and use of design principles that meet both community and technical standards for sound, responsible practice;
- collaborating with other units of government within a region to better integrate transportation considerations across responsible agencies, jurisdictions, and modes;
- planning transportation in cooperation with land use, natural resources, economic development, and other agencies responsible for these community assets;
- including livability as an important goal in transportation planning and measuring the consequences of transportation choices with reference to livability, among the host of factors that go into planning;
- actively using data and crosscutting measures that show the relationships of transportation choices to land use, economic development, and the environment and the potential impacts of these choices on livability;
- using GIS and other tools to support analysis and decision making, emphasizing interrelationships, and making the content and implications of planning information clear to analysts, community members, and decision makers;
- using the 15 metropolitan planning factors, with appropriate supporting information, to develop and assess transportation plans and their impacts;
- implementing active, inclusive community involvement programs as an integral part of the planning and decision-making process, including diverse stakeholders from public officials to users, residents, businesses, civic and special interest groups, and those traditionally underinvolved and underserved;
- incorporating community perspectives and needs via the partici-

patory process; tailoring potential improvements to community goals, and seeking the support and consensus of a broad range of community stakeholders on desirable courses of action;

- using information display and management tools, along with decision-support processes and tools, to better inform all participants in planning (transportation analysts, community participants, and decision makers) and to highlight relevant conflicts and choices that are legitimate parts of analysis and deliberation;

- presenting information so it is clear and useful, both for those with technical expertise and for laypeople, as well as using multiple media, particularly visual displays, to make the meaning of the information clear and unambiguous; and

- making the decision process itself transparent; identifying those important decision points that occur midstream in planning and at key milestones; and specifying who makes the decisions, with what information and input from others, and with what authority and expertise.

REFERENCES

Atkinson, A., and J. Stiglitz. 1980. Lectures on Public Economics. New York: McGraw Hill.

Banister, D. J. 1994. Transportation Planning. Spon, London.

Boulding, K. E. 1974. Reflections of planning: The value of uncertainty. Technology Review 77(1):8.

Copeland, T. E., and V. Antikarov. 2001. Real Options: A Practitioner's Guide. New York: Texere.

Dixit, A., and R. Pindyck. 1994. Investment Under Uncertainty. Princeton, N.J.: Princeton University Press.

Fisher, A., J. Krutilla, and C. Cicchetti. 1972. The economics of environmental preservation: A theoretical and empirical analysis. American Economic Review 62:605-619.

Forester, J., ed. 1985. Critical Theory and Public Life. Cambridge, Mass.: MIT Press.

Forester, J. 1969. The Deliberative Practitioner: Encouraging Participatory Planning Processes. Cambridge, Mass.: MIT Press.

Gavin, Jennifer. 2000. Building livable highways. AASHTO Quarterly (Fall):23-25.

Habermas, J. 1984. Reason and the Rationalization of Society, Volume 1 of The Theory of Communicative Action, Thomas McCarthy, transl. Boston: Beacon Press [originally published in German in 1981].

Habermas, J. 1987. Lifeworld and System: A Critique of Functionalist Reason, Volume 2 of The Theory of Communicative Action, Thomas McCarthy, transl. Boston: Beacon Press [originally published in German in 1981].

Innes, Judith. 1996. Information in Communicative Planning. Institute of Urban and Regional Development Working Paper 679 (October). University of California at Berkeley.

Meyer, Michael D. 1999. Refocusing transportation planning for the 21st century. Presented at Conference on Refocusing Transportation Planning for the 21st Century, February, Transportation Research Board, Washington, D.C.

Meyer, Michael D., and Eric J. Miller. 2001. Urban Transportation Planning: A Decision Oriented Approach. New York: McGraw-Hill.

Nyerges, Timothy. 2001. Panel 4: Data and technology: Tools, access, and decision-making. Data process and tools for transportation decision-making. Presented at National Research Council Workshop on Transportation Decision-Making: Place, Community, and Quality of Life Irvine, Calif., January 29.

Tiebout, C. 1956. A pure theory of local expenditures. Journal of Political Economy 64:416-424.

Weiner, Edward. 1992. Urban Transportation Planning in the U.S.—A Historical Overview. Washington, D.C.: U.S. Department of Transportation.

Zodrow, G., ed. 1983. Local Provision of Public Services: The Tiebout Model After Twenty-Five Years. New York: Academic Press.

If Only Traffic Would Match the Car, 1952, by Art Bimrose. Courtesy of *The Oregonian* magazine.

5

Data and Analysis Tools

INTRODUCTION

Both the results of a decision-making process and the process itself are important in place-based decision making. All stakeholders should be involved in developing the questions that guide the decision making, in choosing the factors included in the planning, and in assessing the outcomes of decision making. This chapter focuses on the data and tools that are required to support sound decision making, that is, to support decisions that both are technically sound and engage the people who are impacted by them.

As seen in earlier chapters, there is no single indicator, or set of indicators, that will work for all transportation and livability issues or in all places for a single issue (Sawicki and Flynn, 1996). Indicators vary with the interests of people in the community. Therefore, indicators are best selected within the context of a particular decision or set of decisions. Similarly, while tools such as Geographic Information Systems (GISs), decision-support systems, and remote sensing are aides to transportation planning, technology cannot choose the problems that are addressed. For tools to address problems, communication must take place among people, transportation experts, technology experts, and governments at all appropriate levels.

This chapter explores the role that federal, state, regional, and local governments, as well as private sources, have played in making data available. It also identifies which gaps exist and what possible steps might be taken to increase the availability of important data to those engaged in discussions about livability in a particular place.

Public data are clearly useful for decision-making purposes, but improvements in the quality and accessibility of these data are necessary. Many federal data creation and delivery programs have provided much useful information to state and local decision makers; however, these programs could be improved by making data available more frequently, for more parts of the country, and at greater resolution. Urban and suburban issues in particular require high spatial resolution and relatively high temporal resolution data, such as traffic surveillance or percentage of impervious surface coverage. State and local data are also useful but could be improved by adopting standards that allow data to be comparable across political boundaries. Much of the data needed by metropolitan planning organizations (MPOs) are geographical in nature and have these inherent scalar integration issues.

If decision making is to be effective, data must be available to the public. However, placing government data in the public domain is not a simple task. For example, much more useful data could be available to decision makers at low or no additional costs if administrative data (usually of a socioeconomic nature such as percentage of children receiving lunch subsidies or families receiving aid in a district) were made accessible to others outside the collecting agencies. However, this would require care in protecting the privacy of individuals who are part of these data, additional security to prevent users from causing problems in the system, and appropriate levels of information and disclaimers so that data are not misused.

Although the broadening of public access to data is essential, improvements in the quality of available data must be made as well. Quality of data refers to the appropriateness, consistency, timeliness, and level of geographic and topical detail. Individuals' ability to access and use data may be limited by lack of access to tools, such as Internet technology, or unfamiliarity with available data, data tools, or methods of data analysis. Accessibility may also be restricted by basic social inequities such as the physical isolation of the elderly. Individuals and groups may be excluded from the decision-making process as well by agenda-setting techniques that expressly or inadvertently make the results of the decision-making process a foregone conclusion (as discussed in Chapter 4).

The federal government, as well as state and local governments, have initiated many programs for collecting and sharing data and for delivering these data to the public. Some state departments of transportation are being given new responsibility for data such as environmental measuring and monitoring, (e.g., streamwater quality and fish passage) rather than having these data collection responsibilities remain the sole responsibility of state and federal natural resource agencies. At the same time, state departments of transportation are delegating other data responsibilities to the private sector. Still, many data collection and data and technology use issues are local in nature. In remarks made at the Woodrow Wilson Center in Washington, D.C., on March 9, 2001, Katherine Wallman, chief statistician of the Office of Management and Budget, identified the following challenges in using federal data for local decision making:

1. *Obtaining reliable data*:
Gathering data that provide reliable information for small (local) areas is extremely expensive. Success requires adequate funding, respondent cooperation with largely voluntary federal requests for data, and education about confidentiality policies to allay public concerns about privacy.

2. *Lack of appreciation for the sources of data*:
There is a lack of awareness of data sources. Statistical agencies have a low public profile. Private sector partnerships with federal data producers and resultant value-added products further obscure the initial federal sources of data.

3. *Organization of the federal statistical system*:
Historically, the development of the federal statistical system in a decentralized fashion has resulted in rich but somewhat inaccessible sources of data. During the past decade, there has been considerable effort to increase the accessibility of federal data, but further interagency coordination and cooperation are essential.

4. *Understanding the data*:
Data that are collected by various agencies, for different purposes, may be confusing to users. Although electronic dissemination has made differences in concepts, constructs, and definitions more obvious to users, informed use of data requires user understanding of data sources, reasons for collection, and data comparability. Initiatives to improve documentation are under way, but more attention is required on this front.

In addition to data, people need access to analytical and decision-making tools. Raw data are rarely useful on their own. Tools are required to summarize data and to determine relationships between inputs and outcomes. The case study, presented in Box 5.1, describes such an effort in the Minneapolis-St. Paul area. The I-35W Corridor Coalition's goals were regional community development, quality growth and diversification, and collaborative planning.

BOX 5.1
Minnesota: North Metro I-35W Corridor Coalition

I-35W is the economic engine for the part of the northeast Minneapolis-St. Paul metropolitan area. However, common development issues throughout this corridor needed to be addressed, and regional and local transportation networks were facing increases in congestion.

Local demographics were changing, the housing stock was aging, and opportunities for infill development and life cycle housing were recognized. The region had to develop a plan to facilitate the shifting economic development patterns and needs. The I-35W Corridor Coalition was established and was devoted to the following vision: "To jointly and cooperatively plan for and maximize the opportunities for regional community development, quality growth, and diversification through a system of collaboration." The coalition established a comprehensive GIS to assist in the build-out study and the development of a regional blueprint.

The coalition represented the member cities of Arden Hills, Blaine, Circle Pines, Mounds View, New Brighton, Roseville, and Shoreview. The coalition partners included representatives from the county, school districts, public agencies, University of Minnesota's Design Center for American Urban Landscape, foundations, and the business community. The coalition included a 14-member policy board of city mayors and managers. The Community Development Director Committee provided

(A) The I-35 corridor. SOURCE: Design Center for American Urban Landscape, College of Architecture and Landscape Architecture, University of Minnesota.

continued

oversight and support for the effort. Special task forces such as those committed to GIS, housing, or transportation priorities were included as needed. Professional staff and community partners supported the effort.

The planning framework was developed by the Design Center. The private sector carried out framework studies, for transportation and housing, and created and maintained databases for GIS and socioeconomic information. The success of the effort was based on building trust between communities. City mayors, managers, and directors met regularly to discuss potential projects that had multijurisdictional impacts. Proactive leveraging of both public and private investments was critical to achieve the coalition's objectives. In addition, collaboration both within organizations and with external organizations, including the private and nonprofit sectors, was needed.

The collaborative planning effort emphasized integrated subregional systems. Information sharing across political and jurisdictional boundaries was required to foster collaboration on common problems and challenges. The coalition recognized the need to have consistent, accurate, up-to-date, complete data and an efficient means of managing, recording, analyzing, and presenting the information. GIS technology was the ideal candidate because more than 80 percent of the data have a geographic component and this tool is powerful and simple to use. The coalition aimed to enable member cities to implement and access data-rich GISs and provide public access to coalition data through GISs. A coordinated and collaborative database and GIS were developed to efficiently share information to encourage consistent and cooperative subregional land use policies.

The data were gathered from various pools, including agreements with counties and cable commissions, secured grants from MetroGIS and the Environmental Systems Research Institute (ESRI) secured contracts from the Office of Commercial Realtors, and reputable GIS sources. The data were purchased and installed into the coalition data server and made accessible on the coalition's web site. A GIS coordinator was hired to gather and prepare base GIS data and the coalition's "On-Line Atlas" was established.

Cities, school districts, county departments, and state agencies submitted valuable data. This information included parcels, existing land use, future land use, generalized future land use, and zoning information. The 1997 Digital Orthophotos, U.S. Geological Survey (USGS) Digital Aerial Images, Federal Emergency Management Agency (FEMA) Flood Insurance information, and building footprints were integrated into the database. Transportation information, such as road edges, traffic assignment zones, and road centerlines, was added to the database. Environmental data included major and minor watersheds, hydrographic information, and the National Wetlands Inventory. Other infrastructure information incorporated into the GIS included county assessor's data, sewer interceptor systems, sewer sheds, and the location of wastewater treatment plants. Socioeconomic data were also integrated into the system. Many layers of text complemented the image data. Parcel and land use data are updated quarterly using unique automated procedures.

The data were compiled to create new demographic building blocks. This initiative required great effort and expense because no current Census data were available for use. A consultant was hired to merge data from schools, voter registration,

continued

BOX 5.1 Continued

ownership records, and municipal utility data to obtain an estimate of the size and age distribution of households. Other social and demographic data were desired, but the data attained were the best available at the time. If current Census data had been available, the coalition would have used that information instead.

When the new demographic building blocks were defined, 5,000 "insight blocks" were created within the corridor. The smallest units of summary (5 to 10 households) were mapped over the entire parcel base. Multiple blocks can be put together to fit any user-defined area to give an overall picture of local needs. These insight blocks do not rely on fixed census or jurisdictional boundaries, and data in the system were more current and more flexible to use than Census data. The Design Center's Livable Community tool for neighborhood and subregional planning was established to address critical needs within communities. These data can be updated frequently to map changing neighborhood characteristics and needs. It was expected that this tool would be applied to life cycle housing analysis, transit and traffic demand planning, economic development planning, and transit linkage between the work force and jobs.

Composition and concentration data of households could be viewed as blocks. Neighborhood profiles were developed from current population and household data. These data were obtained from several state and local databases by cooperative data sharing using county tax and property data, school census data, utility billing data, and driver's license and vehicle registration data. Note that there is no release of confidential data on individuals or households.

The coalition was able to use the GIS software applications and new updated databases to identify and explore subregional patterns and trends. The patterns and trends included land use and transportation, designated town centers, neighborhood corners, the economy and environment, affordable housing, and the presence of nature in an industrial park and mixed-use area. The coalition was able to use this information to augment traffic modeling, calculate density of potential transit users, inventory natural resources, identify housing issues, attract and assist new businesses, monitor redevelopment, and identify community infrastructure. (See map of Arden Hills proposed comprehensive plan in Plate 6.)

The coalition initiated a build-out project discussion. The mission of this project was to achieve regional blueprint goals through subregional collaborative actions in partnership with the Metropolitan Council. This study's approach allowed the subregion to be viewed as a network of local economic, social, natural resource, and infrastructure systems to enhance and implement the regional blueprint. The purpose of this study was to compile a projected 20-year development pattern, clarify complex layers of system and service needs, identify combinations of appropriate "smart-growth" strategies, and provide communication links between local, subregional, and metropolitan partners. The build-out study sought to construct options from local comprehensive plans, assess land use capacity to achieve livable community principles, and conduct subregional market analysis of livable community development types. The effort aimed to coordinate multimodal transportation projects, increase mobility, and assess the implications of municipal actions for subregional and metropolitan systems, such as transportation, transit, and housing.

continued

The coalition has the ability to develop a preferred build-out option, which identifies implementation and financing strategies and develops subregional models of metropolitan communities. Cities can implement regional blueprints at the local level. Subregional collaboration can bridge metropolitan issues and local circumstances. The coalition will assess a transit corridor component to investigate how the regional multimodal network can be expanded into the subregion. One possibility includes acquisition and redevelopment of the local railroad line as an alternative transportation connection and link to other networks. The data, blueprint, and build-out study provided a basis for many alternative plans to be evaluated.

SOURCE: http://www.I35w.org.

DATA AVAILABILITY

Chapter 1 discusses indicators of livability (see Table 1.2). Much of the data mentioned in that table are extant, simple, and useful to transportation planners and managers. However, a major problem with these data is that they are available for politically defined places such as states or municipalities rather than for places defined by other relevant means such as environmental or social considerations.

Data related to flows would be very useful to transportation professionals and other decision makers if there was a reliable, consistent source for such information. Gaps in available data include descriptions of the flows of workers from one part of a metropolitan area to another; how long it takes to make such a trip; and what activities, such as errands, these workers might attend to along the way. Other examples of gaps include data needed for disaster preparedness: although the government provides weather data, it does not provide terrain data that are useful in determining required elevation data resolution for flood control. In terms of transportation decision making, it is difficult to collect data about past patterns of transportation investments. Yet data on the historical precedents of these investments are important as indicators of social equity, as well as sources of information about depreciation and deterioration of infrastructure and about obsolescence in terms of location, safety, and other characteristics.

Federal Government Data

The federal government makes available enormous amounts of valuable data, which are used by all levels of government, the private sector, nonprofit organizations, and individual citizens. We live in an information age; the demand for data and information, as a basis for decision making about economic, social, and environmental issues, is unprecedented. Although the federal government supplies much of these data, people are largely unaware of the sources of the data they want or use. In fact, one federal data source known as FedStat (see Appendix A for federal data sources) uses the Internet to deliver data collected and published by more than 70 federal agencies without the user's knowing in advance which agency produced them. While it may not be necessary to know which agency produced the data, public support for government depends on public understanding of the role that government plays in people's lives. Federal data help us understand how well (or poorly) the economy is running so that we can take steps to improve it. Data tell us about environmental quality so we can take preventive or remedial measures on critical issues and about differential levels of educational attainment and health within our populations so we can increase attention to removing barriers to equality.

Much federal data are available for subnational areas such as regions and states. We know which parts of the country have higher and lower unemployment, air quality problems, and traffic congestion. In many cases, these data are collected directly by or for the federal government. In other cases, data are collected by local or state government, using federal standards, so that uniform data are available across the county. At the county level, data are much more sparse and even more difficult to find in smaller areas. The Census Bureau's American Community Survey (ACS) promises to be a major source of small-area socioeconomic data, but it is still in the process of implementation (see Appendix A). Were this data available, the I-35W Coalition's data collection problems would be simplified. County and subcounty data are currently available from the Census Bureau's decennial Census.

Most data collected by state and local agencies are disseminated and made useful and available by federal agencies, principally the Census Bureau, the Bureau of Transportation Statistics, the Bureau of Labor Statistics, and the Bureau of Economic Analysis. Agency by agency, database by database, federal, state, and local partnerships are essential. Agreeing upon standards is critical to this effort, since data must be uniform across all places to be meaningful in summary and for comparison among places. Especially in the field of transportation, there remain many opportunities for creating standards for data collection and reporting.

There are multiple reasons why federal data are so valuable. They are ubiquitous, by and large available for every place in the country. Federal data are also uniform in nature, and their characteristics are well documented; therefore these data are comparable over large areas of the country. Federal data are generally of high quality, defined as appropriateness, consistency, timeliness, and relevant level of geographic and topical detail. Federal data are essentially available free of charge. Federal rules require that federally obtained data be provided to the public at no cost other than data processing fees. The United States exemplifies a commitment to the distribution of data, especially spatial data at no cost. Many believe our easy access to information has provided public and private organizations in the United States with an enormous advantage in the new economy based on information and information technology.

It is reasonable to think of data as infrastructure in an information age; accordingly, a National Spatial Data Infrastructure (NSDI) was designated by executive order in 1994. A major component of NSDI required all federal agencies to develop plans for making their data available to the public (NRC, 1993, 1994, 1995). As federal agencies amplify their efforts to provide data to the public, data partnership among various levels of government have evolved. Much of this change was driven by federal agencies' realization that insufficient resources were available at the federal level to complete any national data program at a scale that would work for place-based decision making. From the local level, the realization came that cost and work sharing with the federal government was a good way to get the data needed for local decision making.

The NSDI has been enormously successful in providing a wide range of useful data. At the core of the NSDI are seven "framework" data layers: geodetic control, ortho-imagery, elevation, transportation, hydrography, governmental units, and some cadastral information. The original concept spoke of critical thematic data and included such additional data as demographics, soil type, land use, and wetlands. Seven years later we have 1:12,000-scale ortho-imagery for most of the United States, along with 1:24,000-scale digitally scanned topographic maps and a 30-meter digital elevation model (see Box 5.2 for definition of "scale"). Large portions of the National Wetland Inventory are mapped at 1:24,000, and steps have been taken to accelerate the national county soil-mapping program. In addition, the Census Bureau continues to deliver high-quality, high-resolution decennial Census data. The Census Bureau has also conceptualized the new American Community Survey, which would represent a large step in the direction of providing data for place-based decision making.

**BOX 5.2
Scale**

The *American Heritage Dictionary* defines map scale as "a proportion used in determining the dimensional relationship of a representation to that which it represents." If 1 inch on the map equals 1 inch on the earth, the scale is 1:1. Such maps are pretty impractical, and it is typical to have a map representing much more territory in a single inch.

Following the rules of the dictionary, reading the scale as a proportion, geographers and cartographers say that 1:5,000,000 is a *smaller* scale than 1:4,800. Proportions are read as fractions, and the larger the denominator (the number to the right of the colon), the smaller the fraction. After all, $^1/_{32}$ is smaller than $^1/_2$. In daily conversation, we often say "small scale" when we really mean to look at a small geographic area in more detail. To a geographer, this is larger scale. The casual speaker is using *map extent* instead of *map scale*. Because this is a publication of the scientific community, the term *scale* is used correctly to mean:

small scale = less detail, covering a large geographic area;
large scale = great detail, covering a small geographic area.

Sometimes it is better to avoid this semantic problem by talking about coarse versus fine resolution of map detail. This is especially true in the digital age when maps can be printed at any scale. However, paper maps, often the source material for their digital counterparts, have numeric scale and use of scientific terminology is the best way to treat this information.

SOURCE: USGS (2000).

Sample Scales and Typical Uses

Scale	One Inch Covers Roughly	Typical Map
1:480	0.008 mile (40 feet)	Engineering design
1:1,200	0.02 mile (100 feet)	Engineering plans for streets and roads
1:4,800	0.076 mile (400 feet)	City map showing sidewalks and cross-walks
1:24,000	0.38 mile (2000 feet)	U.S. Geological Survey topographic map
1:100,000	1.6 miles	City street map
1:1,000,000	16 miles	State highway map
1:5,000,000	80 miles	Wall map of the continental United States

Data from the NSDI partnerships have been useful to communities across the country, as suggested by demonstration projects conducted from July 1998 to May 2000 by the Federal Geographic Data Committee (FGDC) together with the National Partnership for Reinventing Government and five federal agencies (FGDC, 2000). These projects took place in six communities and dealt with a wide range of issues including crime prevention, land use planning and smart growth, flood mitigation, and environmental restoration. Of course, local data were needed to complement the federal data and address specific issues, and often the federal standards enhanced the ability of a given community to acquire local data from adjacent communities. Several projects in this spirit have been initiated by the federal government, such as the GeoData Alliance, which is a nonprofit organization open to all individuals and institutions using a GIS to improve the health of communities, economies, and the earth (see http://www.geoall.net). However, the GeoData Alliance efforts are still in the early stages of development.

These efforts revealed other problems with the federal data. Most often mentioned was coarse granularity. Data that look detailed from a national perspective are often too coarse to address local issues such as crime, or flooding, or growth. For many community issues, higher-resolution data are needed.

Besides scale, there are five other significant reasons why federal data may be inadequate for local use.

1. *Limited Availability*: Sometimes federal data are not yet available for a particular location. Soil data, useful for many purposes including knowing about construction problems, are a prime example. Despite an accelerated national program, only a small portion of the 3,100 counties in the United States have adequate soil maps.

2. *Timeliness*: This can be a problem for data about phenomena that are changing rapidly. Census data are an excellent example. Decennial Census data are collected only once every 10 years. As one moves further from the census year, the data become more dated and less reliable. For volatile information, Census data may be good 2 two years out of 10. Another example involves digital orthophotos and orthophoto mapping. These are techniques by which spatial data can be more accurately measured and communicated. An orthomap combines the image of an aerial photograph with metrics that allow for direct measurements of geographic location, distance, angles, et cetera. The federal program in orthophoto mapping, led by the U.S. Geological Survey (USGS) and the Natural Resources Conservation Service (NRCS, formerly the Soil Conservation Service), has been very useful for local planning

efforts, but the images show the landscape nearly a decade ago; new images are needed, and plans to update them are uncertain.

3. *Restricted access*: The federal government collects many data for administrative purpose that are not summarized or made available to decision makers, despite the 1994 NSDI executive order. Administrative data are generated from the ongoing record keeping of social welfare and other public agencies and programs. Most of these data could be acquired through the Freedom of Information Act, but the bureaucratic and financial barriers are significant; just determining how to frame a data request can be overwhelming. Examples of restricted data include information about toxic spills into rivers and local summaries of income tax, employment, and welfare cases.

4. *No data*: Some data are critical, but the federal government has no funding for developing data that could be useful for local decision makers. A prime example is that of land use data, which are of significant interest to many agencies but the primary responsibility of none. Therefore, we have never had a detailed national land use map. We get some satellite data, but no systematic classification into land use categories. The USGS has made several short-lived attempts to develop land use data or standard classifications that could be used across the country.

5. *Uncoordinated data*: Interoperability among datasets is limited by the use of different geographies, nonstandard codes, unique computer systems, and narrow visions. Too often, data are collected for a single purpose and are not suitable for comparison with other data. The U.S. Department of Transportation (DOT) is organized according to transportation mode (e.g., Federal Highways Administration, Federal Railroads Administration). In the past, communication among these mode-specific administrations has been limited and highly structured. Although there are some ongoing efforts to facilitate cooperation and coordination among these administrations (e.g., the "OneDOT" program), cooperation with respect to data collection and sharing has been particularly difficult. Data collection, database maintenance, and data quality assurance or quality control are difficult and expensive. The mode-specific administrations have understandably focused past efforts on collecting data for particular purposes. However, integrated digital geographic databases impose new requirements that necessitate new data collection, maintenance and quality assurance-quality control efforts by these administrations. Unless the benefits can be demonstrated to mode-specific administrations, it is difficult to see how they will change their data collection and process-

ing activities. Unfortunately, this is a "chicken and egg" problem since it is difficult to demonstrate benefits without good data.

Other Government Data

The prime responsibilities of most state and local governments do not include data production. Instead they have primary administrative responsibilities that require data collection as part of their day-to-day activities. For example, as part of the property tax system, local governments collect data on housing value that can also be used to monitor inner-city decay or revitalization. Building permits, used to protect the health and safety of inhabitants, can also be used to monitor the spread of the city into the countryside.

In a few cases, state and local governments do gather and publish data for use by others. A number of states have produced detailed land use maps, allowing data to be distributed widely. In the Twin Cities of Minneapolis and St. Paul, regional government cooperated with state government to license current, accurate, street centerline data (including address ranges on all street segments) from a private firm, including access to all state and local government offices, which are accessible at no charge.

There are multiple reasons why state and local government data may be less than ideal. Some of these reasons are discussed below.

1. *Cost*: Cities and states are not restricted from charging for their data, and high costs can limit access to these resources. High-cost data make for uneven access, which becomes an equity issue. However, a reasonable rationale for the sale of data is to cover the cost of creating the database. Cities and states are not mandated to collect and distribute data. They have functional roles, and data distribution is an extra service. It is reasonable for them to charge a fee for those who need those data, but that fee can discourage access for some legitimate users of the data.

2. *Refusal*: Since not all states require that government-collected data be made available to the public, refusal to share data is common. In some cases, privacy restrictions prevent the release of data, but interpretation of privacy rules varies greatly. Another problem is the wide variation in interpretation of federal privacy rules. Federal data about the number of employees at a location are important for transportation planning. (ES202 data are available at http://www.bls.gov/cewover.htm.) Although the State of Wisconsin provides easy access to these data for research purposes, they are not available in many other states. Wisconsin helps protect the privacy

of employers by prohibiting the publication of information about those firms included in the data and requires that researchers be discreet.

3. *Inability*: Much data are stored in older information systems designed for a particular purpose, and these systems are often incapable of providing the data in any other way. For example, a city assessor's system created to produce property tax records might be unable to answer questions about the number of three or more bedroom apartments in a neighborhood. Such basic information is used for estimating population capacity and therefore transportation demand. All the relevant data are in a computer system, but the system was created before commercial database packages were available, and any unique report would require the services of a programmer in a long-forgotten computer language.

4. *Quality*: Data may be incomplete, badly documented, or inappropriate for the intended use. An example is the ES202 employment data (see above) collected by states. Information on employment is collected as part of unemployment insurance programs—information that could be useful for transportation planning. Because those collecting the data are focused on the insurance issue, they do not require reporting firms to adhere to the rule about separating employees by place of work. All 8,000 employees of the Minneapolis public schools, working at more than 100 sites around the city, are reported as working at the school district's downtown headquarters. The data are more than adequate for administration of the unemployment program, but lacking in usefulness for indicating jobs in particular parts of the city.

5. *Lack of standards*: Data from various counties may be of the highest standards, yet collected in nonstandard ways, so it becomes difficult or impossible to compare data across counties. A prime example is travel behavior inventories. These are taken infrequently, and standards are not uniform. Federal standards could help solve this problem.

6. *No data*: The basic parcel map, showing where people live, does not exist in digital form for much of the country. The Western Governors' Association (2001) is working to resolve this problem west of the Mississippi, in cooperation with the Bureau of Land Management. Guidelines, good geodetic control, and some kind of financial support seem to be the necessary ingredients.

7. *Federal paradox*: State and county governments are unwilling to give their data to any activity involving the federal government because the federal government is then required to make the data available to everyone at no cost. State and local governments often

need the funds that come from selling their data to support ongoing system maintenance; if they give their data to the federal government, the market for their information is lost when buyers can get the same information free of charge from the U.S. government.

Private Data

Sometimes private data are the best available. For example, Grubb-Ellis has data available on commercial office space for major markets across the country. Its data include information of total square feet, vacant space, and rents. No government organization has such information. Dun & Bradstreet sells information about firms, their location, and employment. Similarly, Dodge-Polk is the best source of national data about registered motor vehicles. All of this information could be useful in transportation planning. Of course, private information is usually available at a price and users will have to decide whether they can afford it or whether it is sufficiently valuable for their purpose.

Private firms also have significant amounts of data on households and small geographic areas—data that can be useful for direct marketing and other forms of advertising. Included in these private data are current population estimates, estimates of income, and data about expenditure patterns. The population estimates build off previous Census counts and building permit data collected from local government offices. The expenditure data are based on data collected at the point of sale by asking a customer where he or she lives or from analysis of credit card purchases.

Private firms also have qualitative data that they use to determine the needs and desires of communities. Firms such as Claritas have worked hard to develop psychographic profiles of small geographic areas that, together with quantitative data, help organizations determine where to focus their promotional efforts. Some types of people are more likely to favor all-terrain vehicles, and Claritas can help identify communities in which target populations are concentrated (Weiss, 1988, c. 2000). Such data and information have multiple applications for place-based decision making and community planning.

Much of the data held by the private sector already exist in the public sector, but the private sector data are more useful. Data on availability of office space are collected by local government assessors, but Grubb-Ellis's data are more current and comprehensive. Individual states have motor vehicle registration data, but Dodge-Polk makes such data comparable across the country. State governments collect data on employment, but Dunn & Bradstreet data is available for individual firms and location. The Census provides demographic data every 10 years, but Claritas updates its information regularly and adds both quantitative and qualitative data to this base.

Data Collected by Communities and Smaller-Level Governments

Frequently communities must collect their own data because they cannot locate or afford data from others. Most often the factors important to a community concerning a particular issue have not been considered at all by private or government organizations, and data about them do not exist. Citizen attitudes about an issue are one example of such data.

The community is faced with two obstacles as it considers collecting data about these issues. The first is cost. If the issue is important only to that local community, no one else will be willing to share the expense, which could be considerable.

The second issue is quality. Data will have to be of sufficient quality to be credible to other participants in the discussion. If the quality is too low, it will be dismissed. There is the chance that even high-quality data will be dismissed because the issue is deemed irrelevant, so the community might be wasting its money no matter how well it has done its work.

Access to Data and Analytical Tools

Data have no value unless they can be accessed and used. Tools are needed to aid communities in accessing and analyzing data, especially those with limited technical and financial resources. Larger cities and towns are likely to have the resources to be self-sufficient, and smaller cities and larger community-based organizations have taken advantage of falling prices for hardware and software to become self-sufficient as well. However, neighborhood and other community groups typically depend on pooled efforts and the goodwill of others (Leitner et al., 2000; Sawicki and Peterman, forthcoming). Breakthroughs in providing access to data and tools are coming rapidly, but most of this access has been at basic levels that do not approach the sophisticated levels of analysis available to professional planners.

Increasingly, data access is provided over the Internet. For example, Census data are available over the Internet (see http://www.census.gov), and plans call for making data from Census 2000 available over the web, via American Factfinder (see Appendix A). Increasingly, federal, state, and local governments are finding that providing their data free on the Internet saves them the cost of servicing customized requests, while allowing more people access to their data.

A growing number of sites are providing community data and maps via the web. The Geography Network attempts to be a clearinghouse for a wide variety of users and providers of data (for example, the Network provides on-line delivery of demographic data from CACI International Inc., for a geographic area surrounding a user-provided address [see http://geographynetwork.com]). *National Geographic* provides a range of useful maps from its web site (see http://www.nationalgeographic.com). Universities and others are providing on-line access to Census maps and analysis (e.g., the Ralph and Goldy Lewis Center for Regional Policy Studies at the University of California-Los Angeles, which focuses on residential segregation in the Los Angeles area; http://www.sppsr.ucla.edu/lewis/hs~CensusUpdates.html). Many counties provide on-line access to parcel-level maps and data about housing values, recent sales, et cetera (for an example, see http://www.co.dakota.mn.us/assessor/real_estate_inquiry.htm).

Related to Internet access is data provision in kiosks and on mass-produced disks. In all cases, the data provider incurs a substantial cost in preparing the data and documentation for distribution, but then saves money in not having to spend time with each data requestor and customizing a response. Users are given quicker, more consistent, and cheaper access to data.

Data over the Internet (and related technologies) are sometimes attractively packaged with graphs and maps that help users see patterns in the data. Often, however, communities must manipulate and combine data to make sense of them in terms of their own livability goals. The Orton Family Foundation is developing a new land use simulation and visualization program called CommunityViz. This is a rare example of software designed to combine various aspects of community planning and to make the results available to the local community. More information can be obtained at the foundation's web site (http://www.orton.org/).

One of the more difficult problems facing policy analysts, stakeholders, and decision makers is the choice among competing forecasting methods and models. As a case in point, consider land use-transportation models that forecast future travel demands and land uses. An urban or regional system is a web of trends and interactions that evolve at different speeds, ranging from instantly changing subsystems such as travel patterns; to medium-speed subsystems such as workplace and housing locations that take multiple years to change; to long-range subsystems, such as transportation, communication, and utility networks; and land-use, which can require decades to change.

Consequently, land use-transportation models are complex and often require simplifying assumptions for tractability (Wegener, 1994). In addition to data and computer requirements, the choices among land use-transportation models actually includes selecting which "story" you believe about how cities and regions evolve. Policy makers and decision makers often do not have the background or time to evaluate the assumptions, strengths, and weaknesses of these theories of change. The result is that major infrastructure and policy decisions are often based on forecasts from methods whose validity is unknown.

The need to supplement data with description information is well recognized. *Metadata*, or "data about data," allow the user to assess the appropriateness of the data for the task at hand. There are standard templates required by federal agencies and transnational organizations for data. An analogous concept is a *metamodel*, or a "model about the model" (i.e., a high-level [semantic rather than formal] description of the model). This will require developing standardized and understandable metamodel templates for particular modeling domains (e.g., travel demand, demographics, hazards). This information could be delivered within a software environment using the common agent-based technology of *wizards* that guide users through complex software installations or operations.

SUMMARY AND CONCLUSIONS

The federal government plays a significant role in providing data to support decision making at the national and subnational levels. Its various statistical arms collect and disseminate data that are critical for decision making by all sectors and at all levels. Other critical data are collected by state and local governments and reported in a standard form that adds to the data resource base of the country.

Yet there remain gaps in the data, which makes it difficult to make sound place-based decisions. The major gaps include the following:

1. Certain data are not available on a sufficiently timely basis (for example, decennial Census data for small areas). Such demographic data collected only once a decade may have been adequate in an earlier period, but this is no longer true. Proposed changes to the decennial Census, such as the American Community Survey, would provide for the collection and dissemination of smaller-area data on a much more timely basis.
2. Often data is not available at a scale that are adequate for local decision making. Fine-resolution data are collected by state and local government and by private enterprises. However, privately collected data are frequently prohibitively expensive for community use. Also, data collected by state and local governments at finer resolutions could be used more efficiently if national standards were in place. The federal government is in the best position to lead such a standards effort.

3. Data coverage is patchy and inconsistent. For example, only a fraction of the counties in the United States have digital parcel data, and few of those who do have it follow a common standard. Remedying this situation requires additional resources. The Bureau of Land Management (BLM) and the Western Governors' Association are working to remedy this situation, but they struggle with limited resources. BLM has begun to extend this cooperative effort to the eastern states, but it will require even more resources.

4. Land use information is critical for transportation and other planning, yet there is no federal program to provide this information or to define standards for its collection by state or local government. The creation of standards would be the least expensive approach for the federal government to address. Federal support for collection of land use data in communities with limited resources would be needed

5. Some federal data could be quite useful for local decision making, but additional effort is required to clarify collection and distribution procedures. The ES202 data are a prime example. Data are often collected without regard to actual work location of employees. The individual state agencies that collect data under federal guidelines have varying understandings of whether these data can be distributed to anyone outside their individual agencies for any purpose.

6. Federal data programs have to be reviewed and revised because they are incompatible with other federal data collection activities. In particular, the various mode-specific administrations of the U.S. Department of Transportation collect data that are difficult to combine into a general picture of transportation services or needs.

7. The rules making all data "owned" by the federal government free to all potential users limit the willingness of various public and private entities to share data with the federal government. This is counterproductive to good public decision making. Approaches should be pursued to limit these rules where appropriate.

The federal government is taking advantage of developing technologies for distributing data via the Internet, thereby making them accessible to communities across the country. What is lacking is access to robust models that allow communities to see the implications of alternative transportation alternatives. In part, this is due to the lack of public access to easy-to-use models. A more basic problem is the consensus about which models work best in a particular situation. This underscores the need for greater communication among public, private, and professional sectors. Just as private citizens and other decision makers need models to see and understand alternatives, traffic professionals need to interact with academic and technical communities so that they can anticipate tools that may be available in 5, 10, even or 20 years and so that development of the tools can keep pace with emerging problems. This will help communities protect their cultural, environmental, and social resources and plan to meet their own needs and those of future generations.

REFERENCES

FGDC (Federal Geographic Data Committee). 2000. NSDI Community Demonstration Projects Final Report. Available at http://www.fgdc.gov/nsdi/docs/cdp/. Accessed October 1, 2001.

Leitner, Helga, Sarah Elwood, Eric Sheppard, Susanna McMaster, and Robert McMaster. 2000. Modes of GIS provision and their appropriateness for neighborhood organizations: Examples from Minneapolis and St. Paul, Minnesota. URISA Journal 12(4 Fall):43-56.

NRC (National Research Council). 1993. Toward a Coordinated Spatial Data Infrastructure for the Nation. Washington, D.C.: National Academy Press.

NRC. 1994. Promoting the National Spatial Data Infrastructure Through Partnerships. Washington, D.C.: National Academy Press.

NRC. 1995. A Data Foundation for the National Spatial Data Infrastructure. Washington, D.C.: National Academy Press.

Sawicki, David S., and Patrice Flynn. 1996. Neighborhood indicators: A review of the literature and an assessment of conceptual and methodological issues. Journal of the American Planning Association 62(2):165-183.

Sawicki, David S. and David R. Peterman. 2002. Surveying the Extent of PPGIS Practice in the United States. In W. J. Craig, T. M. Harris, and D. Weiner, eds., Community Participation and Geographic Information Systems. London: Taylor and Francis.

U.S. Geological Survey. 2000. Map Scales Fact Sheet 038-00. Available at http://mac.usgs.gov/mac/isb/pubs/factsheets/fs03800.html. Accessed on March 6, 2002.

Wegener, M. 1994. Operational urban models: State of the art. Journal of the American Planning Association 60(Winter):17-29.

Weiss, Michael J. 1988. The Clustering of America. New York: Harper and Row.

Weiss, Michael J. c. 2000. The Clustered World: How We Live, What We Buy, and What It All Means About Who We Are. Boston, Mass.: Little, Brown.

Western Governors' Association. 2001. Western Cadastral Data and Policy Forum Report. Available at http://www.westgov.org/wga/publicat/ cadastral.pdf. Accessed October 1, 2001.

American Community Survey

(http://www.census.gov/acs/www/)

   The American Community Survey (ACS) is a new approach, designed to collect timely information needed for critical government functions. It is an ongoing survey that the Census Bureau plans to use to replace the long form in the 2010 Census. Toward the end of each 10-year Census cycle, long-form information becomes out of date. ACS allows community leaders and other data users to have access to more timely information for planning and evaluating public programs than is available from the decennial Census.

   The ACS will provide estimates of demographic, housing, social, and economic characteristics every year for all states, cities, counties, metropolitan areas, and population groups of 65,000 people or more. For smaller areas, it will take three to five years to produce data. For rural areas and city neighborhoods, or for population groups of less than 20,000, it will take five years to accumulate a sample similar to that of the decennial Census. These averages can be updated every year, so that eventually, it will be possible to measure changes over time for small areas and population groups.

QuickFacts

(http://quickfacts.census.gov/qfd/)

   State and County QuickFacts provide frequently requested Census Bureau information at the national, state, and county levels. This user-friendly web site provides access to multiple datasets.

American FactFinder

(http://factfinder.census.gov/servlet/BasicFactsServlet)

   This provides a search feature of the Census Bureau's web site that helps users locate data quickly and easily from the 1997 Economic Census, the ACS, the 1990 Census, the Census 2000 Dress Rehearsal, and Census 2000. Access to thematic maps and reference maps that include roads and boundary information is available via FactFinder.

Bureau of Economic Analysis

(http://www.bea.doc.gov/)

The Bureau of Economic Analysis (BEA) prepares regional economic accounts for the United States to provide estimates of state and local-area personal income and gross state product. For state personal income and gross state product, BEA's regional estimates are comparable across each region and state, and for local-area personal income, BEA's regional estimates are comparable across each metropolitan area, BEA economic area, and county. BEA's Regional Economic Information system (REIS) is a comprehensive federal income and employment series.

The estimates and analyses of state and local-area personal income and of gross state product are published in BEA's monthly journal, *Survey of Current Business*. In addition, BEA also prepares estimates of regional economic multipliers.

U.S. DEPARTMENT OF HOUSING AND URBAN DEVELOPMENT (HUD)

The mission of HUD is to provide a decent, safe, and sanitary home and suitable living environment for every American. HUD's efforts are aimed at creating opportunities for homeownership; providing housing assistance for low-income persons; working to create, rehabilitate, and maintain the nation's affordable housing; enforcing the nation's fair housing laws; helping the homeless; and spurring economic growth in distressed neighborhoods.

Research Maps (R-MAPS)

(http://www.huduser.org/datasets/gis/gisvol2.html)
(http://www.huduser.org/datasets/gis/gisvol3.html)

Research Maps (R-MAPS) is a set of HUD products designed to democratize housing and urban data, making the data more accessible and usable to researchers, policy makers, and practitioners. The geographically coded data in these CD-ROMs provide Geographic Information System (GIS) data pertaining to a wide variety of housing and urban issues in U.S. localities.

HUD On-Line Bibliographic Database

(http://www.huduser.org/bibliodb/pdrbibdb.html)

The HUD USER database is the only bibliographic database dedicated to housing and community development issues, containing more than 10,000 full-abstract citations in housing policy, building technology, economic development, and urban planning.

Urban Research Monitor

(http://www.huduser.org/periodicals/urm.html)

This newsletter provides a comprehensive list of new housing and community development research, organized by subject from "affordable housing" to "zoning."

U.S. DEPARTMENT OF LABOR

Bureau of Labor Statistics (BLS)

(http://www.bls.gov/home.htm)

BLS provides three types of data for use in place-based and regional planning: labor force status of persons by place of residence; jobs and wages by place of work; and prices and living conditions. The Local Area Unemployment Statistics Program prepares monthly labor force data for 6,700 areas in the United States, including states, metropolitan areas, counties, and cities of more that 25,000.

U.S. DEPARTMENT OF TRANSPORTATION (DOT)

Bureau of Transportation Statistics (BTS)

(http://www.bts.gov/)

Intermodal Transportation Database

(http://www.itdb.bts.gov)

The Intermodal Transportation Database (ITDB) provides a variety of transportation data. These data have been collected by various agencies within DOT and other federal agencies, such as the Census Bureau. The

ITDB is being released in stages. Currently available features include a downloadable center and links to many transportation-related sites on the Internet. The ITDB mapping center includes GIS applications and datasets. The ITDB web site also offers the ability to download numerous datasets containing raw ITDB data. Datasets include airline ontime flight data, population estimates data, hazardous materials, recreational boat accident reporting, and National Transportation Safety Board data.

The Transportation Data Links option provides a one-stop gateway to relevant transportation data and information. Individuals, decision and policy makers, private sector businesses, and organizations can access timely and relevant data.

U.S. DEPARTMENT OF AGRICULTURE (USDA)

The mission of the USDA is to enhance the quality of life for the American people by supporting the production of agriculture. The department carries out this mission by ensuring a safe, affordable, nutritious, and accessible food supply; caring for agricultural, forest, and rangelands; supporting sound development of rural communities; providing economic opportunities for farm and rural residents; expanding global markets for agricultural and forest products and services; and working to reduce hunger in America and throughout the world.

Natural Resources Conservation Service (NRCS)

(http://www.nrcs.usda.gov/)

The NRCS manages many programs to conserve and sustain the country's natural resources. Agents across the country work with farmers and others to develop management plans that yield economic and environmental benefits. Much of this work is based on soil maps, because soil types are so important to crop yields and environmental issues. Their National Cooperative Soil Survey (NCSS) program is a partnership led by NRCS of federal land management agencies, state agricultural experiment stations, and state and local units of government that provide soil survey information necessary for understanding, managing, conserving, and sustaining the nation's limited soil resources.

Soil surveys provide a scientific inventory of soil resources including maps that display locations and extent of soils, and data regarding the physical and chemical properties of those soils. These data provide information regarding potential problems for use of each kind of soil to assist farmers, agricultural technicians, community planners, engineers, and scientists in planning and transferring the findings of research and experience to specific land areas. The Soil Survey Geographic Database (SSURGO) consists of map data, attribute data, and metadata and makes up the most detailed of NRCS data. However, only a fraction of the nation's counties have usable digital soil surveys.

U.S. ENVIRONMENTAL PROTECTION AGENCY (EPA)

(http://www.epa.gov)

EPA's mission is to protect human health and safeguard the natural environment, including air, water, and land, upon which life depends. For 30 years, EPA has been working for a cleaner, healthier environment for the American people.

Smart Travel Resources Database

(http://yosemite.epa.gov:/aa/strc.nsf)

This web site provides information about campaigns that encourage people to make travel decisions that have positive impacts on air quality, congestion, and quality of life. The Resource Center was developed to assist transportation practitioners, public decision makers, industry, consultants, public interest groups, and others who support alternatives to information exchanges about these issues. The center is organized by program characteristics, including location, sponsor, targeted pollutants, program type, and program title. By selecting the category of greatest interest, users can access a list of all applicable program summaries and can subsequently select particular summaries to view or print. Each summary provides information on the program's purpose, theme, development status, basic design elements, and other key features. In addition, there are links to various materials used by the program (e.g., brochures, posters).

Electronic Newsletter from EPA's Information Resources Center

(http://www.epa.gov/epahome/newslett.htm)

The EPA Headquarters Information Resources Center publishes a weekly electronic newsletter that describes environmental information and databases available from federal agencies, state and local governments, academic entities, the private sector, and other sources.

EPA's Envirofacts Database

(http://www.epa.gov/enviro/index_java.html)

EPA's Envirofacts database and mapping applications web site—a single point of access to a wide range of the agency's data—provides access to several EPA databases about emissions, pollutants, and activities affecting air, water, and land in the United States. Users can query the databases individually or search multiple databases. The site also contains associated mapping tools such as EnviroMapper and Query Mapper, which allow users to visualize environmental information at national, state, and county levels.

EPA's Integrated Risk Information System (IRIS)

(http://www.epa.gov/ncea/iris.htm)

EPA maintains this electronic database containing information on human health effects that may result from exposure to various chemicals in the environment. IRIS was originally developed for EPA staff to provide consistent information on chemical substances for use in risk assessments, decision making, and regulatory activities. This information is most useful to individuals who have some knowledge of the health sciences, and it is now available to the public.

EPA's Window to My Environment

(http://www.epa.gov/enviro/wme/)

This web site is a prototype web-based tool that provides a wide range of federal, state, and local data. The information provides visual representations of environmental conditions and features by city and zip code. Among the information available is air emissions, Superfund sites, hazardous waste information, demographic data, and natural features, which can be selected and viewed in combined layers.

U.S. DEPARTMENT OF THE INTERIOR (DOI)

U.S. Fish and Wildlife Service (FWS)

National Wetlands Inventory Center

(http://www.nwi.fws.gov/)

The National Wetlands Inventory (NWI) of the FWS produces information on the characteristics, extent, and status of the nation's wetlands and deepwater habitats. The NWI has mapped 89 percent of the lower 48 states and 31 percent of Alaska. About 39 percent of the data for the lower 48 states and 11 percent of Alaska are digitized (computer-readable digitized wetlands data can be integrated with other layers of the National Spatial Data Infrastructure [see below under interagency sources] such as natural resources and cultural and physical features). These efforts can lead to production of selected color and customized maps of the information from wetland maps, and the transfer of digital data to users and researchers worldwide. NWI also maintains a map database of metadata containing production information, history, and availability of all maps and digital wetlands data produced by NWI, and dissemination of wetlands-related spatial data. These data can be used in a variety of applications, including planning for watershed and drinking water supply protection, siting of transportation corridors, construction of solid waste facilities, and siting of schools and other municipal buildings.

U.S. Geological Survey (USGS)

(http://www.usgs.gov)

The USGS web site provides an enormous variety of materials, including fact sheets, data, maps, reports, and links to other sites of interest. Below are some highlights of the USGS web site.

National Atlas

(http://www.nationalatlas.gov/atlasmap.html)

In the early 1970s, the *National Atlas of the United States of America* was typically found in the reference collections of libraries across the United States. Educators and government organizations were the primary customers for the original publication, but not many Americans were adding the atlas to their home libraries due to its cost ($100). The new National Atlas is designed for individuals and organizations owning personal computers.

The National Atlas includes five distinct products and services. In addition to providing high-quality, small-scale maps, the atlas includes national geospatial and geostatistical data sets. Examples of digital geospatial data include soils, county boundaries, volcanoes, and watersheds. Crime patterns, population distribution, and incidence of disease are examples of geostatistical data. This information is tied to specific geographic areas and is categorized and indexed using different methods, such as county, state, and zip code boundaries, or geographic coordinates such as latitude and longitude. These data are collected and integrated to a consistent set of standards for reliability.

The atlas includes on-line interactive maps. These maps include links to related sites on the Internet for more up-to-date, real-time, and regional data information. The new atlas also includes multimedia maps designed to animate and illustrate change. Finally, the National Atlas includes both documentation for each map layer and articles that describe why the data were collected and how they have been used.

USGS Hydrology Division

(http://water.usgs.gov/data.html)

Water data available on the USGS web site include real-time data from 3,000 on-line stations in the United States. The National Water Information System web site (NWISWeb) includes water resources data for approximately 1.5 million sites in the United States, territories, and border locations, from 1857 to present. Data can be retrieved according to this category, such as surface water, ground water, or water quality, and by geographic area. Of the 1.5 million sites with data, 80 percent are wells; 350,000 are water quality sites; and 19,000 are streamflow sites, of which more than 5,000 are real time. NWISWeb contains about 4.3 million water quality samples and 64 million water quality sampling results. Data are also available on water quality monitoring, sediment transport and associated contaminants in streams nationwide, water use data by county and watershed, and acid rain precipitation and deposition data from more than 200 stations nationwide. (Also see the National Hydrography Dataset [EPA-USGS] under interagency sources below.) GIS data for water resources are also made available at this site.

U.S. GLOBAL CHANGE RESEARCH PROGRAM (USGCRP)

The USGCRP works with research institutions to improve climate fluctuation and long-term climate change prediction. The USGCRP sponsors research of vulnerability to environmental change, including climate, ultraviolet radiation, and land cover.

Gateway to Global Change Information

(http://www.globalchange.gov)

This site provides current news regarding climate change and access to datasets of climate change data. The site contains links to relevant agency programs.

INTERAGENCY SOURCES

The FedStat Task Force

(http://www.fedstats.gov/)

FedStats offers a range of official statistical information made available to the public by the federal government. The site offers Internet links and search capabilities to track economic and population trends, health care costs, aviation safety, foreign trade, energy use, farm production, and more. It is possible to access official statistics collected and published by more than 70 federal agencies without having to know which agency collects them.

FedStats includes MapStats, which allows users to access data according to state, county, federal judicial district, or congressional district. In addition, Small Area Income and Poverty Estimates allow users to locate economic data on the scale of school districts. The Small Area Income and Poverty Estimates program of the U.S. Census Bureau uses models to estimate the income and poverty for states, counties, and school districts during years between Census measurements. A wide array of other state, county, and local-area statistics are available.

Federal Geographic Data Committee (FGDC)

FirstGov

(http://www.firstgov.gov)

FirstGov is a government web site that provides one-stop access to all on-line U.S. federal government resources. The site provides information, rather than "data." FirstGov offers browsing capabilities to a wide range of information from the collections of the Library of Congress to following the progress of a National Aeronautics and Space Administration mission. It also enables users to apply for student loans, track Social Security benefits, compare Medicare options, and administer government grants and contracts.

National Spatial Data Infrastructure (NSDI)

(http://www.fgdc.gov/nsdi/nsdi.html)

The NSDI, established by Executive Order 12906, provides for a consistent means of sharing geographic data among all users to produce significant savings in data collection and provides geospatial data throughout all levels of government, private and nonprofit sectors, and the academic community.

The goals of this infrastructure include reducing duplication of effort among agencies; improving quality and reducing costs of geographic information in order to make geographic data more accessible to the public; increasing the benefits of using available data; and establishing key partnerships with states, counties, cities, tribal nations, academia, and the private sector to increase data availability. The NSDI framework's seven geographic data themes are geodetic control (National Geodetic Survey), ortho-imagery (USGS-NRCS), elevation (USGS), transportation (DOT, USGS, Census), hydrography (USGS), government units (Census), and cadastral information (Bureau of Land Management). NSDI also supplies information regarding community partnership programs.

NSDI Community Demonstration Projects

(http://www.fgdc.gov/nsdi/docs/cdp)

The FGDC, National Partnership for Reinventing Government, and five federal agencies conduct the NSDI Community Demonstration Projects to demonstrate the utility of geographic data for community decision making and the role that federal agencies play in community information needs. The demonstration projects included in the report are Baltimore, Maryland (crime prevention and analysis); Dane County, Wisconsin (comprehensive land use planning); Gallatin County, Montana (Smart Growth); Tillamook County, Oregon (flood mitigation and restoration); Tijuana River Watershed, San Diego, California (environmental restoration); and Upper Susquehanna-Lackawanna Watershed, Pennsylvania (flood mitigation and environmental management).

National Hydrography Dataset

(http://nhd.usgs.gov/)

The National Hydrography Dataset (NHD) is a cooperative EPA-USGS program that provides a comprehensive set of digital spatial data that contain information pertaining to surface water features such as lakes, ponds, streams, rivers, springs, and wells. Within the NHD, surface water features are combined and provide a framework for linking water-related data to the NHD surface water drainage network. These linkages enable analysis and display of these water-related data in upstream and downstream sequence.

The NHD is based on the content of USGS Digital Line Graph (DLG) hydrography data integrated with reach-related information from the EPA Reach File Version 3 (RF3). Based on 1:100,000-scale data, the NHD is designed to incorporate and encourage the development of higher-resolution data.

U.S. Interagency Working Group on Sustainable Development Indicators

(http://www.sdi.gov)

In 1996, the U.S. Interagency Working Group on Sustainable Development Indicators (SDI Group) in Washington, D.C., recognized the importance of monitoring the nation's progress toward national sustainability goals. One goal was to assist the federal government in developing national indicators of progress toward sustainable development in collaboration with nongovernmental organizations and the private sector. The web site provides information, background research papers, and links to data sources. An extensive and well-documented report on indicators for sustainable development in the United States, entitled "Sustainable Development in the United States: An Experimental Set of Indicators," is available.

REFERENCES

Cortright, J., and A. Reamer. 1988. Socioeconomic Data for Understanding Your Regional Economy. Washington, D.C.: Economic Development Administration, U.S. Department of Commerce.

Norwood, J. 1995. Organizing to Count: Change in the Federal Statistical System. Washington, D.C.: Urban Institute Press.

Appendix B

Workshop Agenda and Participants

AGENDA

Workshop on Transportation Decision Making:
Place, Community, and Quality of Life
Arnold and Mabel Beckman Center
Irvine, California
January 27-29, 2001

Saturday, January 27

6:30 p.m.   Welcome Dinner for Participants and Guests

Sunday, January 28

8:45 a.m.   Welcome
              Kathleen Stein, Chair
              Introduction to the study

9:00   Keynote Address
              Speaker: Myron Orfield
              Key ideas and focus of the study

10:00-10:15   Break

Dimensions of Livability

10:15 a.m.	Panel 1:	Dimensions of Livability
	Presenter:	Clinton J. Andrews
	Panelists:	Genevieve Giuliano, Mark S. Henry, and Natalie Gochnour

| 12:00 p.m. | Lunch | |

1:00	Panel 2:	Where the Rubber Meets the Road
	Presenter:	Robert D. Yaro
	Panelists:	Sue McNeil Patricia, Hannah Twaddell, and Patricia Rincon-Kallman

| 2:45-3:00 | Break | |

| 3:00-6:00 | Roundtable Discussion: Common Threads and Emerging Themes | |

| 6:00 | Adjourn | |

Monday, January 29

Pushing the Frontiers

8:00 a.m.	Panel 3:	New and Crosscutting Indicators
	Presenter:	Lyle Wray
	Panelists:	David Sawicki and Shari Schaftlein

| 9:45-10:00 | Break | |

10:00	Panel 4:	Data and Technology: Tools, Access, and Decision Making
	Presenter:	Timothy Nyerges
	Panelists:	Jacky Grimshaw, Daniel A. Rodriguez, Piotr Jankowski, David Sawicki, and Dennis Welsch

| 11:30 | Final Commentators Discussion: Susan Hanson, CloAnn Villegas, Eric S. Sheppard, and Detlof von Winterfeldt | |

| 12:30 p.m. | Adjourn | |

PARTICIPANTS

Clinton J. Andrews, Rutgers University, New Brunswick, N.J.

Carol Brandt, Bureau of Transportation Statistics, U.S. Department of Transportation, Washington, D.C.

Genevieve Giuliano, University of Southern California, Los Angeles

Natalie Gochnour, Demographic and Economic Analysis, Salt Lake City, Utah

Jacky Grimshaw, Center for Neighborhood Technology; Transportation and Air Quality Programs, Chicago, Ill.

Susan Hanson, Clark University, Worcester, Mass.

Mark S. Henry, Clemson University, Clemson, S.C.

Piotr Jankowski, University of Idaho, Moscow

K. Sue Kiser, Federal Highway Administration, California Division, Bureau of Transportation Statistics, Sacramento

Sue McNeil, University of Illinois at Chicago

Susan Mockler, National Research Council, Washington, D.C.

Timothy Nyerges, University of Washington, Seattle

Kirsten Oldenburg, Bureau of Transportation Statistics, U.S. Department of Transportation, Washington, D.C.

Myron Orfield, Metropolitan Area Research Corporation, Minneapolis, Minn.

Patricia Rincon-Kallman, City of Houston Planning and Development Department, Texas

Daniel A. Rodriguez, University of North Carolina, Chapel Hill

David Sawicki, Georgia Institute of Technology, Atlanta

Shari Schaftlein, Washington State Department of Transportation, Olympia

Eric S. Sheppard, University of Minnesota, Minneapolis

Hannah Twaddell, Thomas Jefferson Planning District Commission, Charlottesville-Albemarle Metropolitan Planning Organization, Virginia

CloAnn Villegas, Intertribal GIS Council, Pendleton, Ore.

Dennis Welsch, City of Roseville, Minn.

Detlof von Winterfeldt, University of Southern California, Los Angeles

Lyle Wray, Citizens League, Minneapolis, Minn.

Robert D. Yaro, Regional Planning Association, New York, N.Y.

Appendix C

Identifying Data for Place-Based Decision Making

AGENDA

Meeting of Committee with Federal Agencies

The National Academies
National Academy of Sciences Building, Room 250
2101 Constitution Avenue, N.W.
Washington, DC 20418
February 5, 2001

8:30 a.m. Welcome
Kathleen E. Stein, Committee Chair

8:45 Review of the Day's Agenda
Lisa M. Vandemark, Study Director

9:00 a.m.-3:00 p.m. Presentations from Federal Agencies

9:15-9:45 a.m. Bureau of Labor Statistics
John Galvin

9:45-10:30 Census Bureau, U.S. Department of Commerce
John Kavaliunas, Leo Dougherty

10:30-10:45	Break
10:45-11:30	Bureau of Economic Analysis, U.S. Department of Commerce *Hugh Knox*
11:30-12:00 p.m.	U.S. Department of the Interior *Paul Dresler*
12:00-1:00	Lunch
1:00-1:30	U.S. Environmental Protection Agency *Stacy Fehlenberg*
1:30-2:00	U.S. Department of Housing and Urban Development *David Chase*
2:00-2:30	Economic Research Service, U.S. Department of Agriculture *Richard Reeder*
2:30-3:00	U.S. Geological Survey *Hedy Rossmeissl, Dave Kirtland*
3:00-3:15	Break
3:15-4:30	Subcommittee Discussion (CLOSED SESSION)
4:30	Adjourn

PARTICIPANTS

Daniel K. Cavanaugh, U.S. Geological Survey, Reston, Virginia
David E. Chase, U.S. Department of Housing and Urban Development, Washington, D.C.
Leo B. Dougherty, Census Bureau, U.S. Department of Commerce, Washington, D.C.
Paul Dresler, U.S. Department of the Interior, Washington, D.C.
John Eltinge, Bureau of Land Management, U.S. Department of the Interior, Washington, D.C.
Stacy Fehlenberg, U.S. Environmental Protection Agency, Atlanta, Ga.

John Galvin, Associate Commissioner, Bureau of Labor Statistics, Washington, D.C.

John C. Kavaliunas, Census Bureau, U.S. Department of Commerce, Washington, D.C.

Hugh W. Knox, Bureau of Economic Analysis, U.S. Department of Commerce, Washington, D.C.

Richard J. Reeder, U.S. Department of Agriculture, Washington, D.C.

Acronyms

ACS	American Community Survey
AVIRIS	Airborne Visible InfraRed Imaging Spectrometer
BEA	Bureau of Economic Analysis
BLM	Bureau of Land Management
BLS	Bureau of Labor Statistics
BTS	Bureau of Transportation Statistics
CO_2	Carbon dioxide
ComPlan	Interactive land use-transportation computer model utilized
DLG	Digital Line Graph (USGS)
DOC	U.S. Department of Commerce
DOI	U.S. Department of Interior
DOT	U.S. Department of Transportation
EPA	U.S. Environmental Protection Agency
EPI	Eastern Planning Initiative
ES202	Employee Statistics 202
ESRI	Environmental Systems Research Institute
FEMA	Federal Emergency Management Agency
FGDC	Federal Geographic Data Committee
FHWA	Federal Highway Administration
FTA	Federal Transit Administration
FWS	U.S. Fish and Wildlife Service
GASB	Government Accounting Standards Board
GDP	Gross Domestic Product
GIS	Geographic Information System

GNP	Gross National Product
GPI	Genuine Progress Indicator
GWA	Greater Wasatch Area
HUD	U.S. Department of Housing and Urban Development
IRIS	Integrated Risk Information System (EPA)
ISTEA	Intermodal Surface Transportation Efficiency Act
ITDB	Intermodal Transportation Database (DOT)
LEM	Location Efficient Mortgage
MAUP	Modifiable area unit problem
MPO	Metropolitan planning organizations
NAFTA	North American Free Trade Agreement
NCSS	National Cooperative Soil Survey Program (NRCS)
NEPA	National Environmental Policy Act
NHD	National Hydrography Dataset
NO_x	Nitric oxides
NRC	National Research Council
NRCS	Natural Resources Conservation Service (USDA)
NSDI	National Spatial Data Infrastructure
NWI	National Wetlands Inventory (FWS)
NWIS	National Water Information System (USGS)
QGET	Quality Growth Efficiency Tools
REIS	Regional Economic Information System
RF3	Reach File 3 (EPA)
R-Maps	Research Maps (HUD)
SDI Group	U.S. Interagency Working Group on Sustainable Development Indicators
SSURGO	Soil Survey Geographic database (NRCS)
TEA-21	Transportation and Equity Act for the Twenty-First Century
USDA	U.S. Department of Agriculture
USFS	United States Forest Service
USGCRP	U.S. Global Charge Research Program
USGS	U.S. Geological Survey

Index